Strategic Risk Leadership

Modern risk management as practiced today faces significant obstacles—we argue—primarily due to the fundamental premise of the concept itself. It asserts that we are mainly dealing with measurable, quantifiable risks and that we can manage the uncontrollable by relying on formal control-based systems, which has produced a general view that (enterprise) risk management is a technical-scientific discipline. *Strategic Risk Leadership* offers a critique of the status quo, and encourages leaders, executives, and chief risk officers to find fresh approaches that can help them deal more proactively with what the future may hold.

The book provides an overview of the history of risk management and current risk governance approaches as prescribed by leading risk management standards, such as COSO and ISO31000. This enables practitioners to challenge the frameworks and improve their adoption in practice introducing sustainable resilience as a (more) meaningful response to uncertain and unknowable conditions. The book shows how traditional thinking downplays the significance of human behavior and judgmental biases as key elements of major organizational exposures illustrated and explained through numerous case examples and studies.

This book is essential reading for strategic risk managers to understand the requirements for effective risk governance practices in the contemporary and rapidly changing global risk landscape. Indeed, it is a valuable resource for all risk executives, leaders, and chief risk officers, as well as advanced students of risk management.

Torben Juul Andersen is Professor of Strategy and International Management at the Copenhagen Business School and Director of the Global Strategic Responsiveness Initiative. He has previously held executive positions at Citibank/Citicorp Investment Bank, SDS Securities, Unibank, and PHB Hagler-Bailly and is an Honorary Fellow at the Institute of Risk Management (IRM). Torben has also authored numerous books and academic articles on strategy and risk management topics.

Peter C. Young holds the 3M Endowed Chair in International Business at the University of St. Thomas, Opus College of Business and is Director of the Risk Leadership Initiative. He was previously the E. W. Blanch Senior Chair in Risk Management. Peter has been a Visiting Professor at City University, London and Aoyama Gakuin University, Tokyo, as well as Distinguished Honorary Professor at Glasgow Caledonian University. Among many awards, he has received the ALARM-UK Lifetime Service award.

Strategic Risk Leadership

Engaging a World of Risk, Uncertainty, and the Unknown

Torben Juul Andersen and Peter C.Young

 Routledge
Taylor & Francis Group

LONDON AND NEW YORK

First published 2020
by Routledge
2 Park Square, Milton Park, Abingdon, Oxon OX14 4RN

and by Routledge
52 Vanderbilt Avenue, New York, NY 10017

Routledge is an imprint of the Taylor & Francis Group, an informa business

British Library Cataloguing-in-Publication Data
A catalogue record for this book is available from the British Library

Library of Congress Cataloging-in-Publication Data
Names: Andersen, Torben Juul, author. | Young, Peter C., author.
Title: Strategic risk leadership : engaging a world of risk, uncertainty, and the unknown / Torben Juul Andersen and Peter C. Young.
Description: Abingdon, Oxon ; New York, NY : Routledge, 2020. | Includes bibliographical references and index.
Identifiers: LCCN 2019046430 (print) | LCCN 2019046431 (ebook) | ISBN 9780367436308 (hbk) | ISBN 9781003006220 (ebk)
Subjects: LCSH: Risk management. | Leadership.
Classification: LCC HD61 .A535 2020 (print) | LCC HD61 (ebook) | DDC 658.15/5—dc23
LC record available at https://lccn.loc.gov/2019046430
LC ebook record available at https://lccn.loc.gov/2019046431

ISBN: 978-0-367-43630-8 (hbk)
ISBN: 978-1-003-00622-0 (ebk)

Typeset in Sabon
by Swales & Willis, Exeter, Devon, UK

Contents

Acknowledgements

First—and foremost—I would like to extend all my love and gratitude to Sian, my wife. We have shared a journey for over forty years and it is hard to even identify any aspect of my life where she has not provided a positive, steadying, and engaged presence.

Beyond that it almost goes without saying that I am sincerely grateful for my professional association and friendship with my co-author, Torben Juul Andersen. We became acquainted over fifteen years ago when I took on a project in Denmark related to public sector risk management, and—naturally enough—as professors interested in risk management it was inevitable that we would encounter each other. Initially, it seemed that our perspectives were so different that it was difficult to imagine the two of us buckling down to work on something together. But as it turned out we actually decided rather quickly that our differences might prove helpful. I can certainly say that his scholarly reputation and extensive experience in strategic management and international business were highly valued by me. We talk about luck in this book and I can say that I consider myself very lucky indeed to have met Torben and worked with him. We have ideas for the future too.

As one ages, I suppose we all hope that our lives come into a sharper focus. Patterns and progressions may emerge, and sometimes key influences and events come more clearly into view. I emphasize here (in the spirit of our book) the 'I suppose we all hope' segment of that first sentence. There is a lot of murkiness to life and we are—inevitably—struggling as much with uncertainty and the unknown as we are with things in front of our face. Still, in my case, it has become clear that three people have had dramatic effects on my life—so much so that I am compelled to single out each of them for thanks.

The first of these is Donald Norris, my master's degree advisor, who set me on the course of an academic career in risk management. Beyond pointing me in a particular direction Don taught me to respect my (meager) talents and to develop a professional and academic approach to my work. Don and I only worked together for two years in the early 1980s, but here I am—nearly forty years later—riding the wave he initiated.

Second, my PhD advisor, C. Arthur Williams, served as a steady, engaged, and immensely intellectual guiding hand. Along the way he sharpened my academic and intellectual capabilities, but the thing that always stands out in my memory of Art was his profound decency. In his day, he was a dominant figure in the academic world of risk management and insurance, and indeed, he was a significant figure at the University of Minnesota where he provided leadership in a variety of ways (stepping in as business school dean on an emergency basis, redesigning the employee pension system). I am not directing aspersions to any individuals in particular when I say that decency is not always seen in higher education, but Art had it in spades, and his example has always been in my mind when interacting with colleagues, students, and others.

Third, for quite different reasons, I would mention Peter Sylow, whom I first met almost twenty years ago. Peter was then the CEO of Kommuneforsikring, a major insurance company in Denmark. Peter represents, I suppose, the practitioner side of risk management in my career, and it was through him that I became involved in a range of public sector risk management initiatives and projects—initially in Scandinavia, but ultimately throughout Europe (and elsewhere). He is a real intellectual and an innovative thinker, attributes that served him well as an effective executive. Fortunately, he remains one of my very good friends today and continues to be an enthusiastic supporter of mine. He has retired but remains fully engaged in the world of risk management and insurance and I highly value his perspective. Oh yes, and I should mention that our get-togethers commonly involve some of the best wines in the world—and a chance to also visit with his wonderful wife, Aase.

Peter C. Young
Minneapolis

I simply have to acknowledge the unwavering support of my wife, Mette, and the achievements of our children, Christine and Christian, as the fundamental backing and driving forces without which my engagement in writing this book would hardly have emerged.

It is also clear that the current form of the book would never have appeared without the very constructive interactions with my insightful and experienced co-author, Peter C. Young. Peter and I met some fifteen years ago during one of his several outstays in Copenhagen. And in the interim period, we have—fortunately for me—had many opportunities to discuss risk management practice and its development at different events from joint teaching endeavors to conferences and seminars involving practicing risk managers. These many encounters over the years have also had the added benefit of bringing our wives, Mette and Sian, together with us at various social occasions.

Yet, the real trigger point for this book was an invitation from Peter that I spend a semester at St. Thomas University (STU) in Minneapolis among other things with the intent to write an updated book on modern risk management and its leadership features as a way to join our diverse experiences in the field. My visit at STU also received the support of my Department Head, Jens Gammelgaard, at the Copenhagen Business School (CBS) for which I am grateful.

As described elsewhere, the book writing exercise turned into a somewhat different project than initially envisioned, reflecting a very fruitful process of collaborative idea generation that challenged the way we usually think about risk, risk management, and enterprise risk management, and which eventually turned into the present book. I truly appreciate the opportunity to engage in this—for me—rewarding work with a very productive writing process not least due to the eloquence of my co-author. I am quite pleased with the outcome—if nobody else is.

Torben J. Andersen
Copenhagen

Foreword

This is not the book we intended to write. We have wondered how frequently this occurred with authors, and in thinking about it found that Charles Dickens reportedly observed that he sat down at his desk each day wondering what his characters would do next, suggesting that even he could surprise himself. We are going to take some comfort in that.

We had a reasonably solid idea about what we wanted to do at the outset. This was going to be a fairly conventional academic monograph on the challenges of integrating risk management into overall strategic management. Without going too far into the weeds describing what we did not do, it does seem—on reflection—that the book we did write not only was the book we were meant to write, but it actually was the embodiment of our views in action. Most notably, managing the future is tricky. One might have a plan with expected outcomes, but they invariably encounter what actually happens and the choice then becomes to adapt, forge on, or give up. We chose to adapt, which unsurprisingly becomes a central insight of the book—sustainable resilience as a core intention of risk management.

Let's get into this a bit. Through the process of collaborating and corresponding, we began to see that our initial themes themselves rested on other themes and that it was those underlying stories that were really what was motivating us to write. So, while we began by writing on how Enterprise Risk Management (ERM) might be stretched to accommodate particular subjects of interest to us (strategic risk management, risk governance, risk leadership), we slowly began to see that while it was possible to tack these things onto a conventional exploration of modern risk management, we began to realize that ERM was, perhaps, the wrong starting point for thinking about what risk management was supposed to do. Eventually we concluded we had been trying to make a case based on a premise we did not support.

This realization set us down a road—a bit of an uncomfortable road—to determine why we had come to this conclusion. Inevitably, we came to believe that we would have to very carefully explain any argument we did develop. So, as we began in a new direction, we quickly saw that the book could become an exercise in provocation, bomb throwing, iconoclasm—potentially inciting hostile reactions. We did not quite get to the 'Everything you know is wrong' stage, but we weren't far away. That realization really tempered our thinking. How do we make the case that some of the most fundamental beliefs in the risk management world deserve a critical appraisal without coming across as troublemakers? The answer is 'carefully.' In the end, we concluded we did not want to start a revolution; we just wanted to encourage some thinking about issues we deem to be putting extraordinary stress on the foundation of modern risk management.

OK, so much for the build-up. This book sets out to make the case that the way we think about risk management today is the result of a path-dependent process over the past seventy years that—while supportable in many of its details—is nevertheless not the result of a persistent, rational, methodical process. That story involves circumstance, happenstance, contingency, reactive responses to moments of great challenge, and—well, you get the idea. As a result, modern risk management is based on a premise that—we strongly believe—warrants a very critical reassessment. For example, and not to give away the book's big surprises, we believe we have gotten the purpose of risk management the wrong way around. We are in the *uncertainty* business, not the *risk* business. Perhaps this sounds clever, or at least glib. We intend to argue that it changes the role of risk management (and the knowledge, skills, and abilities of risk managers and leaders) in very fundamental ways. And, as will become evident at various spots in our book, we assert that risk management is fundamentally a moral enterprise. Partly we assert this because values matter, but also because the inability to quantify or monetize uncertain phenomena means that our only rigorous *decision rule* is our values.

Along the way we invariably will offer some pointed criticisms of the ERM idea, COSO and ISO (two prominent bodies that are shaping modern views of ERM), some academic theorizing, 'received wisdom,' and even the human brain. If you knew us better, you would realize we are lovely guys, and you would be shocked to hear us talk and act that way about anyone or anything. So, let us be clear here. We respect all those who have contributed thought, toil, and treasure to the advancement of risk management. In particular we would note that while COSO and ISO may occasionally come across as the bogeymen of our book, we don't feel that way—and indeed, we would declare that those two bodies' revisions in recent years are praiseworthy.

Nevertheless, understand that there are many ways in which we humans can't help ourselves. We have brains that trick us, that mislead and impair our ability to think critically. We live in societies that shape the way we perceive the world, but sometimes impede our ability to assess the world we encounter. We are humans—we make mistakes, we can be obstinate, we can be insupportably confident in our own brilliance, we can be fearful, greedy, lazy, venal, petulant ... and more. It never hurts to challenge ourselves. Is what we are seeing true? Is what we are thinking the result of careful analysis? How might we be wrong? Indeed, how might we ourselves be a critical source of risk and uncertainty?

That last sentence suggests another important theme in our book. Understanding human perceptions and behavior are the center point of risk management. Failing to appreciate and act on that is the road to ruin.

OK, what else do readers need to look for?

There are, perhaps, three additional points to flag. First, we have a bit of an obsession with time. It may be that we are getting older, but more to the point here, we see an inherent fault line running through risk management that derives from humans' seeming incapacity to think critically about the long run. And, even if that is possible to do so in particular situations, there is a decided difficulty in sticking to a long-run plan, or a common purpose, once it has been identified.

We can look at any newspaper and point to evidence of this; debates over the climate threat; under-investment in disaster/emergency response capacity; inadequate investment in infrastructure; short-termism on Wall Street. We will argue that many of the most critical risks and uncertainties have this long-run aspect—they are threats in the distant future, or they take a long time to reveal themselves, or we don't have an adequate understanding of the implied risk or uncertainty. Add to this, of course, existing incentives and disincentives to pay attention to the long run, political factors, often highly technical elements that make understanding a challenge, and human nature. So, we do not think we need to make the case that humans have a hard time thinking about and acting in the interests of the future. Modern life itself has made the case for us.

Add to this the fact that—at least conceptually—risk management is by its very nature a long-run project. At its simplest level, it consists of actions taken in the present to address possible events in the future. At a slightly elevated level, the operation of a risk management program seeks stability over the long run. As just one example, insurance buying can be seen as trading unpredictable but large payments (loss events) for small regular payments (premia). And then, of course, risk assessment challenges organizations to shine a light on the unknown future and unearth details that will motivate organizations to focus on improving resiliency.

As we note in the book, risk management has a decided orientation toward the long run but operates in a short-run world. Can anything be done about this? We offer numerous thoughts but recognize the great difficulties and barriers to success.

Second, history matters. This actually appears in different forms in our book, but the main point to make here is that risks and uncertainties live in the past, not just the present and future. Further, as our emphasis on narrative and stories suggests, there are ways to remember the past and to incorporate that understanding into present day analysis. Our Chapter 3 is, largely, a story—the story of how modern risk management came to be. Many people know the highlights of that story, but one of the things we learn here is that the story of risk management was not written by Charles Dickens (oh, that it were) or any single author. The story of risk management, in fact, has many authors and has been formed by many extraneous influences. It is a story, because it hangs together; this happened, which led to this, and then to this and this. However, the plot engine, if you will, is contingency. And as a result, we cannot look at present day statements/standards/declarations about risk management as the inevitable result of a plot line that was developed at the inception of risk management in the late 1940s.

In our focus on history, we do not go too far down the road to get to the concept of institutional memory, but it sits in the background. So, while we have the readers' attention, let us just mention that in addition to being able to build a story that explains how an organization arrived at a given situation in the present moment, someone needs to remember this story. We have had our own observed experiences with organizations that—for whatever reason—essentially lost their institutional memory (lay-offs, M&A, a wave of retirements, etc.), and we can say that if you don't quite believe that institutional memory is important, just look at an organization that has lost it. *Forgetting* can be a source of risk or uncertainty, but *remembering* is a risk management asset.

Third, we see risk management as primarily a 'way of thinking.' It is possible that this is a rather difficult idea for many to process—not because it is overly complex, but rather because it is not easy to think about thinking.

We can say that this was not an early insight for us. After looking at the history of risk management, exploring the standards of practice, puzzling through the differences between espoused ERM and ERM adopted in practice, and beginning to consider an approach to risk management more in line with our views—a moment arrived when we stopped and asked ourselves: What do we observe when we discover an individual manager, department, or organization that 'manages risk effectively'?

This led us to break the function down into its most elemental level, and it is there we concluded that the risk management we 'see' (insurance policies, lumbar support belts, safety training programs) are really just expressions of a *point of view*. That point of view, we believe, is the essence of risk management; what it *is*. This is actually not a simple statement. At a basic level, it suggests that a person has a rather solid grip on the concepts of risk, uncertainty, the unknown, complexity, and has an ability to think critically about them and the ways they can and do influence the organization. In the course of developing that grip, a manager would have to be conversant (we think) in behavioral psychology, organization culture/behavior, and be able to talk meaningfully with technical risk experts (credit risk managers, investment management specialists, and so on), but also have some hold on the much less quantitative side of risk management.

We could scale that idea up and say that this capacity should be a feature of the organization as a whole, and we suppose in many senses this would—ideally—be true. However, one issue we encounter in our exploration of risk management systems and processes is that an integrated command-and-control approach rarely seems to work. Indeed, puzzling through this observation we have come to the realization that responsiveness, resilience, innovation, adaptation most effectively occur in organizational frontlines and this leads us to thinking that all managers and employees have to take this risk knowledge on board and then be empowered to employ it to address the changing world they encounter. Although it is not a prominent point of our argument here, this does suggest that teaching, training, and developing risk awareness among managers and employees might very well be the primary activity our risk leaders/managers would have to take on.

A final comment here regarding our style. It has been argued for decades that writing for an academic audience requires a different approach or writing style than does writing for a business audience. We think some of this is just plain silly but do recognize that the rigors of academic writing and the peer-review process have led to meaningful expectations on how scholars present their case.

We talked about this extensively as a basis for deciding our own approach—which, of course, required us to think about the audience we intended to reach. Recognizing that 'shooting for the middle' yields its own punishment (nobody reads it), we nevertheless felt that the subject matter, the timing, and importance of the issues we discuss pushed us toward a kind of middle ground. We wanted our book to have a foundation based on rigorous, peer-reviewed work, but also did not want business professionals to be put off by the sometimes dense and stilted language of the academy. If you asked us directly, we would say that we think this book could serve well as a supplementary reading in an MBA or Executive MBA course (risk management, strategic management, general business, management accounting, corporate finance), but at the same time could easily be picked up by interested upper level managers. At least, it is our aspiration to make the text equally helpful to both audiences. The proof of the pudding is obviously in the eating, so we will see how things fare, but we sincerely hope the book will be able to provide relevant and stimulating reading to the right people.

1 Is this a risk management book?

When life strips off all her finery, what remains is fortune. Everything that happens is a constant collision of tossed dice.

Roberto Calasso[1]

We see Roberto Calasso's quote as a rather precise description of what humans are up against when it comes to managing risk. It is particularly relevant to our book, for over the span of time since the Classical Greek era, history has—in effect—produced an inversion of Calasso's statement. How did this happen? A study of the history of ideas might begin to answer that—we are not going to pretend that our book can serve as a substitute. Let us just say that—by the end of the 15th century—the stage was set for a rapid acceleration (through the Renaissance, the Reformation, and the Age of Enlightenment, the Industrial Revolution, into the modern age) in humankind's ability, desire, and willingness to describe and understand our uncertain world; to come to measure some aspects of that uncertain world with increasing levels of accuracy; and to slowly reorient us to the view that ours essentially is more a *risky* world than an *uncertain* one. This most certainly applies to the field (academic and professional) of *risk management*, the subject of our book.

A technical clarification here. We define risk as *measurable uncertainty*, so risks are a special category of uncertainty where it is possible to gather observations, or rather where observations have been assembled for analysis (or in recent centuries, developed through theoretical methods) to quantitatively estimate future outcomes. Uncertainty is—well—everything else.

Back to Calasso. His book is an imaginative restructuring of Greek mythology. Are we, therefore, suggesting that our book will be a demonstration of modern mythmaking? Well, we are not cultural anthropologists, but we would argue that science and mythology both seek to explain the mysteries of our existence. In that sense, we see them as endpoints on a continuum and not as distinct unconnected ideas. Thus, a challenge will be to view this imagery as a specific frame of reference risk management must adopt. In doing so we may come to see mythology as a method of illumination that can tell us a great deal about how we should think about uncertainty (and risk). For example, establishing explanations of an uncertain world through narratives will make an appearance in our book, as will the sense that careful thinking about such stories can tease out the distinction between *truth*, *accuracy*, and *meaning*. In other words, a slightly relaxed view of the idea of mythmaking allows us to shine a light on a more expansive means of introducing rational approaches to seeing and explaining our uncertain world.

Having said that, let us be clear. As modern-day scholars we support all efforts to increase our abilities to assess and analyze our uncertain world. Without doubt, our ability to better anticipate the future is one of the reasons for advancement in standards of living over the last 300 years; particularly in the fight against disease, hunger, poverty, unsafe conditions, and insecurity. However, we have come to recognize that the human record on actually converting uncertainties into risks is pretty pitiful when we consider the vast array of things that cannot be quantified. Thus, a central feature of our thinking about risk management is to focus primarily on uncertainty and—let us throw in something that we will explain later—unknowability.

Uncertainties, by definition, are unmeasurable (or, at best, are somewhat measurable or are awaiting future measurability), and that attribute presents the problem of employing consistent and rational analytical processes. In response, we have had to challenge ourselves to develop our argument on two fronts: 1) that the modern view of risk management should be centrally focused on uncertainty, while 2) acknowledging that in recognizing the centrality of uncertainty we will need to battle energetically against the forces of superstition, prejudice, fear, greed, and faulty perceptions. In other words, we sit in the critical thinking camp; a camp that rejoices when we have the capacity to add precision to our thinking about risks, but that also believes we should widen our lens to consider risk assessment to be just a special category of a larger task—assessing the uncertain and unknown. Later we will develop the notion that risk management is primarily a way of thinking, and this paragraph provides a small glimpse into our reasoning.

The risk management guidances, COSO and ISO 31000, will come in for some critical analysis later in this book, but we want to be fair and note that, for example, ISO's recent 2018 update does seem to reveal an emerging view that is consistent with ours.

> Risk is now defined as the "effect of uncertainty on objectives", which focuses on the effect of incomplete knowledge of events or circumstances on an organization's decision making. This requires a change in the traditional understanding of risk, forcing organizations to tailor risk management to their needs and objectives—a key benefit of the standard.[2]

We return to Calasso once more before moving on. The Calasso quote provides us an additional clue as to where our book is headed. His statement offers no particular sense of *progress* or the *narrative arc of history*. Things just happen; the dice clash over and over again. This feels alien to our own time where the Enlightenment (among many influences) has led modern sensibilities to an abiding belief in progress. And, as will be seen, risk management is very much a modernist-progressive project—we are engaged in taming a hostile world, and we aspire to shine an improving light on a future that is better than the present. It is an admirable project and, honestly, we are all for it. Improvements in the lives of humans have given us the privilege of envisioning an even brighter future. We hope humans never lose that sense of optimism.

But from our narrower examination of risk management, we have to say that the image of clashing dice probably more accurately depicts the day-in-day-out life of the practicing risk manager—with no illustrations of that fact being more vivid than the dramatic and extreme events that headline our daily news. Among many key observations, we will wonder why that hope for a brighter future does not lead to humans demonstrating an easy ability to envision the long run (and, as importantly, to stick with any long-run plan that might emerge). In exploring this particular issue, we will encounter the subjects of values, beliefs, behavior, and culture as matters of critical importance.

Before setting out this chapter's introductory description of the present-day scene and teasing out a set of insights that will serve as building blocks for the rest of the book, we want to translate our opening statements into a more subject-matter-specific declaration of our views on uncertainty, supplementing that with a short sidebar look at the issue of time.

UNCERTAINTY IS THE NAME OF THE GAME

Let us begin here by noting that our primary dilemma in writing this book is that the term *risk management* is not really an accurate description of what we will be discussing. While we have decided to stay with that appellation, we also realize that such a decision presents us with certain problems. Notably, continuing to employ the term serves to confuse those who have come to define risk management in its more traditional forms. However—we confess—we are stuck on this.

Given this self-imposed constraint, we will aspire to make the case that the management of risk aligns with only a very small part of what goes on in the world of risk management. Yes, for some risk managers in financial institutions a sizable part of their work involves the manipulation of large data sets, but for most individuals toiling in the field, well, they are working against uncertainties and—here is that word again—unknowabilities. Does this really matter? Does it matter if a risk manager conceives the job as primarily an attempt to view or conceive of uncertainties as risks? Perhaps not in the particularities of risk management practices, but as we will show there is a strong human tendency to mentally convert uncertainties to risks (and convert risks into certainties) even when the volume and quality of information suggests that employing the word *risk* is not warranted and indeed may harmfully influence our thinking. So, although our argument will need to be carefully made, we believe there is an important difference in starting from the view that we exist in a world of uncertainty and that we are obliged to bring a high degree of skepticism to any proclamation that we can take a quantitative risk assessment at face value.

And further, even on rare occasions where we might be able to come close to saying something has become a risk (such as, insurance market data or market data for financial derivatives), we would have to note that there are very clear illustrations of elegantly produced, data-abundant risk modeling destroyed by 1) the unexpected/unmeasurable, non-modelable and 2) the gullibility that we demonstrate by our uncritical acceptance of the results produced by a quantitative risk assessment exercise. We offer four words in support of our view—the 2008 financial crisis. Note that even well before this extreme event occurred, Nassim Taleb had identified the elephant in the room, which he referred to as a 'Black Swan' phenomenon.[3] And to this day he continues to remind us that, "We are managed by small (or large) accidental changes, more accidental than we admit."[4]

For just one more time let us be clear—we support the earnest quest to quantify and otherwise measure our uncertain world. Better understanding of our complex world should always be applauded. However, human perception and behavior under conditions of uncertainty can wreak havoc; a point that may be acutely relevant even when dealing with huge data sets and complex assessment methodologies. Intelligent data analyses can help us manage more effectively, but quite often they can also lead us into trouble.

Clearly, the right response is NOT to close our eyes and pretend that 'soft' issues that are hard to measure do not exist. As Carlo Rovelli concludes: "The temporal relations between events are more complex than we previously thought, but they do not cease to exist on account of this."[5] They do exist (indeed, we argue they dominate), they are truly impactful, and if we don't take them seriously we encounter trouble—unless we are lucky. We will later have something to say about luck too.

There is one additional thing to note regarding risk/uncertainty/ unknowability. It is our contention that organizations mainly encounter uncertainties, but additionally this engagement seems particularly pronounced the higher one scales the organizational ladder. Adequate data—wherever it can be found—tends to reside in the more operational levels of organizational life. Phenomena such as work-related injuries, currency fluctuations, product defects, and data breaches frequently present managers with useful data that allows for assessment and more focused decision making (but even then …).

However, top managers—while clamouring constantly for more data—really operate almost completely in a world of uncertainty. They rarely have enough information to make strategic decisions, and in fact, we might go so far as to say that they are also frequently confronting the *unknown* rather than the *known*. This produces a slightly paradoxical and troubling effect in its own right—the less available the data, the more desperately managers cling to whatever data they can find.[6] It is partly for this worrisome insight that the *risk leader* phenomenon (a concept we explore later) has emerged in recent years. There are other reasons, of course, including regulatory and legal requirements, but we see the essential motive is to place someone in an elevated position to oversee all efforts to assess and address risk and uncertainty. To provide risk/uncertainty expertise, judgment, and insight, if you will.

Sidebar: risk, uncertainty, and the long run

This sidebar may seem, at least at first, a bit incidental to the preceding discussion on risk and uncertainty. However, it sets out an insight that is emblematic of a range of issues that come front and center in our way of thinking. Provocatively, we would phrase the issue this way: 'Does the long run matter?'

Contemplating this question requires us to hold two thoughts in balance: 1) of course it is worthwhile to value and plan for the future, while also believing that 2) hardly anybody ever sticks with it (and to be fair, the high complexity of our modern world may absolutely bar the chances of sticking with it). We do not want to appear polemical here, but there is fairly significant research suggesting that humans generally have difficulty with the concept of time, which becomes particularly vexing when considering time over an extended period.[7] It would be nearly insulting to readers to elaborate too much on this as it is obvious to most that, for instance, a dollar on offer 50 years from now will not possess the same value as a dollar put on offer in the present. In business schools this idea is encoded in the concept of the time value of money, which—to be honest—is both useful but also very much misused.

Note also that the long run often comes faster than one should think—indeed, the lifetime of firms seems to be shortening. So, yes, we believe that thinking about the long-term and sustainable aspects of the business is important, both for equity owners, but also for society at large. Yet, there is precious little evidence of working, successful long-term commitments while evidence of short-termism abounds. At any rate, while there is an important argument to be made about the effects of this phenomenon on headline-grabbing issues like the global climate, we choose here to narrow the discussion to a more functional level. Simply put, risk management can be characterized as involving the expenditure of resources in the present to offset some potential loss in the future.

Even when considering opportunities, we see that initial investments must be made to enjoy a possible future pay-off. The fact that probabilities are at the center of risk management decisions only adds to the challenge. Short-termism may be a vexing challenge for our world, but at the same time, it must be said that time itself is grist for the risk management mill. We could even put it more simply: In the face of short-termism risk management assumes (must assume) an abiding interest in long-term commitments to risk responses and remedies. We believe this is an inherent dynamic tension in both the study and practice of risk management.

Yes, the issue of time exists at the center of the risk management 'idea,' but there is also an interesting risk practice-specific issue. As we will illustrate, organizations themselves have difficulties maintaining risk management programs for long periods of time, though achieving stability over the long run arguably is a central purpose of risk management. We intend to recount several cases of highly regarded risk management programs being abruptly dropped or quietly suffocated for reasons that have nothing to do with the success or failure of that program. Organizational leadership changes, altered circumstances (new competitors, for example), changes in strategy, new acquisitions— all have been seen as factors in the demise of seemingly effective risk management programs. The irony, as we will note, is that the core intention of risk management is based on anticipating and managing those sudden changes, surprises, black swans, and fat-tail events; but even risk management itself can be felled by the exact thing it is commissioned to 'manage.' Could it be that part of the issue is the present day focus on risk rather than uncertainty?

THE CURRENT RISK MANAGEMENT SCENE

We now set the stage for our book by outlining a set of key ideas and providing something of a roadmap for where we plan to go. First, we offer a brief introduction to where risk management is today. Be aware that in the next chapter we examine the journey of risk management from the early days to the present in greater detail.

The history of risk management could be summarized as a journey from a collection of loosely affiliated technical risk functions to something approaching a very large set of better integrated or coordinated risk-handling processes, with more transparent reporting, decision making, and auditing trails than were evident in the earlier versions.[8] This statement is, admittedly, an over-simplification, but it does underscore the fact that today's risk management efforts are traceable through a highly path-dependent historical evolution. We know this should not be particularly surprising, but it arguably gives rise to the following question: Is it possible to set aside the accumulated assumptions, frames of reference, and structures and look at risk management from a different perspective? It is difficult to fully do such a thing, but we believe that the effort in attempting to do so may allow us to tease out the key elements of a response. For now, however, the question at hand simply is this: What do we *say* that modern risk management is, how does it look, and what is it supposed to 'do?'[9]

The 'standardization' phenomenon

Various risk management guidelines and related vocabularies were introduced after the turn of the millennium to create the backdrop for the currently prescribed practices. COSO (*Committee of Sponsoring Organizations of the Treadway Commission*) was formed in 1985 by five professional accounting and auditing entities to counter fraudulent financial reporting.[10] COSO published a number of internal control frameworks in the 1990s and then commissioned PwC to extend this work by developing a view on broader enterprise risks. The result was published as *Enterprise Risk Management: Integrated Framework* in 2004. Note here the introduction of the term Enterprise Risk Management (ERM), which will be fully explained later.

We might also mention that an early risk management guidance was released by the *Institute of Risk Management* (IRM) in 2002,[11] which was subsequently adopted by the *Federation of European Risk Management Associations* (FERMA). But perhaps more significantly, ISO (*International Organization for Standardization*), which was established in 1947 as an international standard-setting body promoting proprietary commercial standards, turned its attention to risk management. The ISO/IEC Guide 73 from 2002 outlined the vocabulary for use in risk management that was applied in the *Overview of Enterprise Risk Management* published by the *Casualty Actuarial Society* in 2003. The Australian and New Zealand risk management standard AS/NZS 4360 from 2004 was subsequently integrated and extended into the ISO 31000 *Risk Management: Principles and Guidelines* in 2009.

These various initiatives—and many other contemporaneous efforts— have collectively provided the foundation for current thinking about risk management of which the most prominent, or predominant, undoubtedly are COSO and ISO 31000. Both have been recently updated and will receive significant attention in our book.

What we see in organizations today

Organizations often have quite diverse and widely deployed risk management practices. The overarching term for these various functional areas (or subfields) is traditional or technical risk management (TRM). Populating the TRM world are several prominent and not-so-prominent specializations. Insurance-buying and threat management are possibly the oldest technical areas to fall under the risk management heading, and even today many define risk management that way (e.g., insurance-buying and managing insurable risks). Financial risk management (FRM) is another subfield addressing issues related to fluctuations in financial markets, e.g., volatile interest rates, foreign exchange rates, commodity prices, etc. Project risk management (PRM) deals more specifically with risks associated with implementation of large public or private projects. Business continuity planning (BCP) refers to a set of processes aimed at preventing effects from break-down of productive infrastructure including fixed assets, machinery, processes, computer systems, and operations in general.[12] Recent additions to the subfield list have focused on supply chain risks, IT risks, emergency/disaster response, and more. The professional individuals active in all these fields are often organized around related interest groups, or associations, that constitute engaged and committed fora of likeminded people.[13]

For many years, these subfields operated largely independently of one another—and often still do—but a growing recognition that greater interconnectivity might be beneficial led to the development of enterprise risk management (ERM) frameworks. ERM represents an attempt to establish a comprehensive, holistic approach to managing all types of risk. This was a shift away from what was often referred to as a 'silo' approach where each of the risk functions was handled separately, and toward an attempt to see risk management as an institutional value-creating activity.

Hence, the aim of ERM was to assess enterprise exposures in an integrated manner across functional areas and coordinate the responses to deal with all the risks, where individual effects may cancel out, be contained, or exploited. The coordination role is often vested in a central office possibly headed by a chief risk officer (CRO, or when we need to employ a more generalized term—*Risk Leader*) with reporting responsibilities to the governance level and direct access for executive and board liaison. Relatedly, the board might also designate a risk committee to support their risk oversight responsibilities.

Risk governance is an associated, but relatively newer—even more loosely defined—concept, referring to how the board of directors guides, authorizes, optimizes, and monitors the risk exposures of the enterprise. It represents an all-encompassing set of tasks and responsibilities that should consider the organization structure, resources, capabilities, financial reporting, process controls, internal auditing, management information systems, etc. It also considers the cultural aspects of governance that enable executives and directors to exercise their oversight roles. In principle, good risk governance provides proper accountability, authority, reporting, and communication mechanisms.

What is risk management supposed to do?

First, it is useful to briefly note that the traditional (TRM) risk management view of its objective was one of mitigation of threats. And, for firms that have not yet engaged in an ERM-oriented approach, loss control might very well remain the overarching objective of risk management. The emergence of the ERM concept served to challenge that objective as being too narrow and disconnected from the broader objectives of value maximization. It should be said that ERM's awareness of the objective-altering consequences of its conceptual premises were not well-understood in the early years. In fact, there is a part of the ERM story which might be seen as involving a retro-fitting of a rationale to align with actual study and practices.

Ultimately, the objective of ERM-influenced risk management is—broadly stated—to add value to the firm/organization, or as CAS states: "increasing the organization's short- and long-term value to its stakeholders."[14] Value creation is the primary objective for directors whether we consider value to shareholders or value to the wider group of core stakeholders. Importantly, this is where the terms *risk appetite* and *risk tolerance* enter the picture.

These concepts have come into vogue in the corporate risk governance and accounting communities. The precise meaning of these terms is still somewhat inconsistent in practice. A common description of risk appetite could be a statement regarding the amount of risk an organization is willing to accept to pursue its long-term objectives, whereas a risk tolerance statement expresses limits for risk (and activities) outside of which the organization cannot/should not go.[15] The idea is that decision-makers throughout the organization can be guided by these statements and make better risk-return trade-off considerations and thereby avoid excessive exposures to secure a proper risk adjusted return on commitments that are made.

The deployment of risk management methods and measures

All the risk management frameworks—without exception—incorporate a simple four-step risk management cycle consisting of: 1) identifying the risks, 2) assessing the risks, 3) treating the risks, and 4) monitoring the risks. The model can vary somewhat in format and posture, but the essential processes are the same, and the supporting tools are quite similar. So, the underlying rationale is that by being aware of the environment it is possible to think through in advance what might impact us and, as far as possible, what necessary precautions may be taken to avoid major loss effects while being able to exploit opportunities.

The process of risk identification is expected to be compatible with the risk appetite statement in view of the strategic objectives and operational goals reflecting the risk attitude of the owners/shareholders (and stakeholders) whose aim is to create enterprise value and enhanced stakeholder benefits. A number of risk classification schemes may be useful in the risk identification process, e.g., considering different types of hazards, financial/economic risks, operational risks, and strategic risks. No particular risk classification framework can claim superiority, but they all are intended to help the risk manager consider possible risk factors and avoid overlooking the obvious and the less obvious risks.

The assessment of risk is analytical and can become somewhat technical. It entails analyses of the identified risks including estimation of possible effects and subsequent evaluations to prioritize the various risks. It is argued this provides a better understanding of the sources of risk events and their eventual influence on strategic objectives, corporate performance, and economic returns. In turn this provides the background for some type of risk mapping exercise, where plotting the potential impacts against the probabilities of occurrence serves as a basis for identifying as first priorities those risks with the highest potential effects.

Risk treatment will apply to those risks that are considered high priorities out of the many risks that are identified. The idea is to focus attention and resources toward the major risks as opposed to getting lost in a dense and rigid register of potential risk events. For each of the prioritized risk events there are essentially four possible ways or outcomes of dealing with the exposure: 1) avoid the risk, 2) transfer the risk, 3) reduce (or mitigate) the risk, or 4) retain (and manage) the risk. The risk treatment decision should be coherent with the risk appetite statement, the overarching strategic objectives, and the associated performance goals.

Risk transfer is relevant in the case of pure downside risks whereas speculative risks entail trade-offs between losses and gains so hedges to stabilize future cash flows can be employed. It might make sense to consider possibilities of reducing the exposure by changing or moderating certain aspects of the business, which can be determined in relatively straightforward cost-benefit analyses.

The retained risks basically remain in the enterprise for ongoing management. They can be consciously retained because they are consistent with the formal risk strategy, or they are retained because they were not identified. As Shimpi argues, "A risk neglected is a risk retained."[16] But the idea is to identify, transfer, hedge, monitor, or otherwise manage key risks, while retained risks are variously subjected to management approaches, including measures to even assume more risks in the essential areas of business competence to optimize the value potential. Since many managers view risk management through a historical lens, it might be assumed that risk management is essentially about threat management. However, as has been noted, one of the central hallmarks of modern risk management is the integration of opportunity management (so-called upside risks) into the overall risk management effort.

As part of the analysis and decision-making component, it is standard practice to apply some form of simulation techniques (Monte Carlo, for example) to gain a better feel for the distribution of possible outcomes as a function of stochastic and erratic input factors that reflect the uncertain conditions.

All of this really captures the essential logic and related practices of modern risk management. Add to this the more recent extensions of the ERM frameworks, including consideration of the so-called 'three lines of defense.' Here the basic idea is to delegate risk responsibility within approved limits to the operating entities that handle the daily business as a first control post. At the same time, a central function will report all the relevant aggregated institutional exposures on a regular basis to the executive and governance levels for oversight purposes as a second control or command post at the center. Then add to this the independent internal (and possibly external) auditing functions for retrospective reviews of the risk processes and practices as a third control post.

... and therefore

While the preceding paragraphs provide a short form overview, they arguably do capture the essential warp and woof of how risk management is practiced today and contain the key ideas espoused therein. And, as it appears, all the proposed processes and techniques apply to circumstances where we can identify the future risk factors in advance, thereby developing satisfactory information about their possible future developments and hence an implied ability to control things going forward. Yet, as we have already argued, there are obviously many factors that are not really risks at all but are more properly understood as uncertainties or phenomena that simply cannot be foreseen. So, how do we handle, or at least anticipate, these potentially influential factors?

That is where the Calasso quote strikes a chord with us. The description of current risk management practices is all about managing *risk*. But, where do we find the organized efforts focused on the uncertain and the unknown (the collision of tossed dice)?

As our discussion so far implies, there must be good reasons why we should consider risk management to be valuable for organizations. As noted, one rational economic argument is that managers should consider investment opportunities based on the expected cash flows and the risks and uncertainties associated with them. So, investors and capital markets will be willing to supply funds for those value-creating investments if they are convinced that the risks are or will be properly managed.

This seems a reasonable position to take, but does it mean then that implementing an ERM-style framework will do the trick for us? Well, not necessarily it seems. A recent study finds "no evidence that application of the COSO framework improves risk management effectiveness."[17] For one thing, the study found that implementation of ERM was not motivated by value-increasing objectives, but was primarily influenced by regulatory requirements, ownership structure, organizational size, and industry context. Further embedded in this finding was the sobering revelation that there is no consistent direct evidence that ERM adds value to the firm.

Needless to say, we intend to examine this issue in some detail, but we are compelled to start our examination from the assumption that the proof of ERM's effectiveness is—well—yet to be established, leading us to ask two questions. One, do the motives reported for adopting ERM tell us something about commitment and support for risk management? And two, are we looking at—or measuring—the wrong things when the presence of ERM is interpreted as evidence of effective risk management? In other words, adherence to ERM—by focusing on handling identifiable risks while saying relatively little about how organizations should deal with the uncertain and unknowable—may lead to measuring the wrong things.[18] A few scholars have put some thoughts to this, including Aswath Damodaran, who adds that effective risk management would likely entail more proactive risk-taking initiatives.[19] Damodaran further suggests the possibility of exploiting a number of 'risk management' advantages that may:

- Generate superior knowledge.
- Enable acquisition of better information.
- Develop speedier observations and insights.
- Engender the ability to react (or act) faster.
- Provide learning and adaptive skills.
- Generate experience dealing with risk events.
- Enable (more) appropriate resources.
- Organize (more) resilient structures.
- Create operational flexibilities.
- Form a capacity to change course.

This is all very plausible and sensible, but it is obviously much easier to state these aims than to impose and execute them in practice. And to be fair to the ERM frameworks, most do mention the importance of risk awareness among all employees in the organization, noting that the tone at the top, the culture, and the organizational climate in which the daily business is conducted are important features in the risk environment. But, exactly how are we supposed to make all this work?

The boundaries of risk management

One of the real conundrums in the study of risk management is that it is—very plausibly—part and parcel of everything that can affect organizational performance. As risk and uncertainty are central conditions of our world, is it really something that can be compressed into a specific managerial function? Just consider a couple of simple examples:

1. A manager reviewing the resumé of a prospective employee, investigates the evidence (calling references, checking former employers), and then interviews the candidate. From this the manager develops a set of questions, including:
   a. Is the person being truthful?
   b. Can I discern that individual's critical thinking abilities?
   c. What is the likelihood that this person is a good fit for the firm?
2. A public works director asks questions in the process of developing the upcoming annual budget for road repairs:
   a. What do we need to do?
   b. How much will we need?
   c. Can we define the consequences of not repairing roads? And, can we live with them?
   d. How long should the repairs we make last?

Our question here is this: 'What part of these two small scenarios is NOT risk management?' If we take the view that risk management is really about the efforts taken to consciously look at and understand our non-certain world and to take steps—with some level of consistency—to address these potential outcomes—well—everything *is* risk management.

   We think a pretty compelling case can be made that this is true, and yet, sitting at our desks preparing to teach MBAs about risk management, what is that syllabus going to look like? After all, as with almost all business school classes, we are preparing people for future careers in management, so the content needs to be subject to summarization, practically presented with relevance to the workplace, and—we suppose—it should be marketable. Oh, and it must fit into a 14-week semester.

   Michael Power cautioned against the 'risk management of everything' tipping over into the 'risk management of nothing,' and we see his point.[20] Partly in response, and after struggling with this issue over the years, we have come to the conclusion that risk management is not a function *per se* (though there are, of course, many functional aspects); rather it is a way of thinking—it is *critical thinking* in the service of interpreting our complex and non-certain world. Readers have seen and will continue to see discussion around this point; critical thinking is a *leitmotif* in this book.

As just a side comment here, the academic literature on risk management underscores the ubiquity of risk and risk management. It is safe to say that almost every field of study—from anthropology to zoology—has a research focus area in risk and risk management. And thus, it is nearly impossible to present a truly comprehensive view of the academic treatment of the subject. Awareness of that fact creates, we think, a healthy state of mind for those in the risk management field (skepticism), and it does seem possible, with some care, to reflect those wide-ranging perspectives in making risk management decisions.

A CHANGING RISK LANDSCAPE

We are keen to get to the development of our ideas in the subsequent chapters, but it is necessary to place the preceding discussion of risk and modern risk management in the context of the wider changing risk landscape and then to offer some speculative thoughts on how we see that changing landscape influencing risk management. In all this we set forward some fundamental ideas that will provide the structural support for the following four chapters.

The trend toward more international organizations with intense cross-border commercial and financial flows, and with social links between geographically dispersed individuals—all of which are bound together by digital technologies—creates the backdrop for a truly turbulent global business environment. This setting can be seen to constitute a *complex dynamic system* comprised of many interacting agents and entities where ongoing changes in multiple places can lead to outcomes that defeat simple comprehension. Further, these effects are *nonlinear* and do not derive from simple aggregation of individual behaviors. The observed events follow often *irreversible* paths where previous decisions influence the options available.

In this environmental context it is impossible to accurately—or even meaningfully—forecast developments because things are intertwined in intricate ways across a multitude of interacting elements. Yet, the organization will still have to deal with events as and when they arise—even though the context defeats the principles of diagnosis. Things happen in new ways that make simple pattern recognition irrelevant as a prescriptive response—new data analytic methodologies notwithstanding. In short, the risk landscape is moving from a *modernist* toward a *post-modernist* perspective.[21] This is also the context for potentially 'rare and improbable' events to exert more influence than we care to believe.

Given this, we may even call into question the authority of so-called *experts* whose scientific knowledge may be confined to very specific knowledge fields—we will come back to this particular point later. As a consequence, it seems we can no longer depend fully on conventional definitions of rationality, on quantification, and on specific risk probability distributions—everything is being challenged. Indeed, it may be that risk itself comes to be seen as only a subjective social multilevel phenomenon that manifests itself as a common belief or view.

This puts us in murky waters, indeed. Are we saying that nothing is certain, everything is relative and subjective? We suppose at a metaphysical level that probably is true, at least within the limitations of human cognition. And it does jibe with our view that risk is just a special category of uncertainty. Nevertheless, we leave metaphysics to the philosophers. There must be something firm that we can hold on to.

WHERE DOES THIS ALL TAKE US?

Chapters 2 through 5 will methodically develop our overarching argument, but for scene-setting purposes, what is the case we hope to make? In brief, we envision a 'repurposing' of risk management. Risks or uncertainties can be hard to quantify and, yes, possible responses must be learned anew every time. In this complex dynamic environment, developments are to a large extent unpredictable and organizations must respond through ongoing learning processes often guided by ethical yardsticks. This learning process can lead to creativity and spontaneous innovations that arise in unpredictable ways—and they can produce a reservoir of potential future solutions. The so-called repurposing that we see as resulting from the existential conundrum is this. While we think the technical goals of risk management are certainly to minimize loss and maximize gain, really, the abiding goal must be to move an organization toward *sustainable resilience* in the face of a highly complex, uncertain, and confusing world.

Resilient organizations arguably prepare for the worst and impose standards to take rapid responses as risk events occur, but this will still require more than standard procedures. Resilience thrives on support and commitment, involvement and interaction, availability of resources, capabilities, and a creative space that can drive innovation, adaptation, renewal, and recovery in the face of extreme and abrupt changes.[22] In organizations this is also influenced by structures, processes, and guiding values including decision-making structures, information processing systems, individual incentive schemes, and so on. Resilience, in this sense, can be conceived as the outcome of recursive processes of sensing, learning, and adaptive innovation that essentially depend on the engagement of open and interactive individuals.

Some conceptualizations or definitions of organizational resilience refer to "maintenance of positive adjustment under challenging conditions such that the organization emerges from those conditions strengthened and more resourceful" in the face of errors, scandals, crises, shocks, and ongoing risks.[23] Note here that the underlying mechanisms that drive this resilience appear linked to individual beliefs and social cognitive processes where past success is treated lightly, whereas the potential for unexpected events receives a high level of attention. The upshot here is that, we are facing a changing environment where impactful incidents are becoming increasingly abrupt, extreme, and unpredictable, which calls for new approaches to deal effectively with risk, uncertainty, and unexpected developments.

And, oh yes; we contemplate that the word *sustainable* has at least two meanings within our view: 1) sustainable in the sense of conscious efforts to consider and address an organization's impacts on people and the environment; but also 2) in the sense of the long-term survival of that organization.

Here we come to the nub of the matter (at least the nub of a particular matter). How do we organize ourselves to take on this task in a complex environment? One idea may be to develop a central function to think through the interrelated risk factors much in line with the enterprise-wide risk management perspective. However, we must realize that this approach has distinct limitations. True, efforts to survive in this world may require more conscious thinking about organization structures and built-in flexibilities. Yet, this handling of implied strategic and operating structures raises tough demands on managerial and executive capabilities. Studies in operations management suggest that central coordination combined with decentralized information sharing is superior in dealing with unpredictable conditions.[24] So, while an instinctive response to high uncertainty might be to centralize, adopt a command-and-control approach, and batten down the hatches, it seems that a more open, decentralized, and—let us say it—trust-based approach could lead to a more verifiably successful response.

Organization studies of *robust* designs for optimized outcomes and *adaptive* designs that allow the organization to modify business activities point to *decentralization* as a way to deal with dynamism and uncertainty. The *delegation* of decision power enables the local operating managers who have the detailed situational insights to make faster and better-informed decisions. Yet, this cannot stand alone—effective organizations have structure—so, combinations of central and decentralized processes are associated with superior risk and performance outcomes. Hence, it is argued that *dynamic adaptive systems* in organizations build on combinations between fast responses in decentralized operating entities and slow forward-looking analytical thinking at the corporate center.[25] This is relatively new ground that needs further experimental research and empirical testing, and we will consider these issues later.

A specific focus on longer-term sustainable effects of organizational actions can help uncover otherwise unobserved long-term threats and opportunities that increase our ability to respond to future risk events in a more timely manner. Recall here, however, the considerable challenge of persisting in the pursuit of long-term efforts. Still, it seems that corporate responsible behavior can enhance the risk responsiveness as positive economic spillover effects improve reputation and reliability. This, in turn, can lever support from essential stakeholder relationships—especially in the context of unexpected crises.[26] The implication, we believe, is a possible evolution toward a more effective enterprise-wide risk management approach that considers the importance of *cultural*, *moral*, and *behavioral* aspects—as opposed to a predominant focus on process optimization and controls—to reach at a higher level of risk resilience.[27]

While core values in the organization are influenced by the actual behaviors of senior management, they and other leaders also determine whether the organizational climate is conducive to creative solutions and innovative responses. Leaders often say they learn from failure, but their actions may still show a preference for success, which will impede organizational learning.[28] These types of individual executive biases may cause all managers to pay attention to what they expect or want to see, so it fits the desired belief of their mental model. Hence, individuals, groups, organizations, communities, and societies typically underestimate the need to prepare for low-probability high-impact—that is, 'extreme'—events. We generally tend to focus on near-term problems dismissing the possibility that disaster can strike tomorrow while quickly forgetting the lessons from previous bad events. This can lead organizations into doing nothing—things are highly uncertain, and nobody else is doing anything either.[29]

We have already noted that we think risk management is or reflects a 'way of thinking,' (conscious, critical thinking), and though this may sound slightly flimsy, this insight serves as the foundation of our larger view of risk management, so it will be up to us to provide meat to the bones. The core challenge is to develop a capacity within all employees and managers to think critically about the phenomena of risk, uncertainty, and the unknowable future. This task is herculean ('Sisyphean' would be the pessimistic term), but without the effort, human nature will continue to intrude on any measures taken to manage risks. We will provide several case illustrations that, cumulatively, set forward the idea that humans—their perceptions and reactions, their motivations, their judgment, the problems with processing the bewildering complexities of our world, and their values (or lack thereof)—can and do play havoc with the most scientifically and precisely designed risk management systems. Risk management starts with people—then moves to systems, processes, controls, and modeling.

So, it should be obvious now that we believe most significant problems and risk management failures are due to human nature. Mind you, sometimes there are pure bolts-from-the-blue. However, in most cases even if we must dig deeply after an event to determine where mechanical causes yield to human factors, we are pretty sure that you will find them. Thus, we look at our focus on human nature as an essential feature of our view. We believe that moving people toward a more conscious and critical understanding of risk, uncertainty, etc. is the fundamental task of risk management. And, by the way, those that might call the management of human factors the 'softer side' of management, would be well advised to acknowledge that if it is 'softer' (read 'easier'), why do so many managers fail to successfully address it?

Will this effort ultimately result in total success? No. We are talking about human beings here. We forget, we misremember, we get lazy, we do not pay attention, we are distractible, and in some instances we are grasping, fearful, and even deliberately amoral. The point is not that our view guarantees a clean-up of all human behavior; neither are we seeing this view as leading us to risk management nirvana. No, our point is that unless we see human behavior as the central focus of risk management, no elegant system, process, guidance is going to paper over the influence of human nature on the best of our risk management intentions.

... and looking ahead

A few signposts for coming chapters. Our view is developed from the idea that modern risk management has driven itself into a *cul de sac* as the result of path dependency and thus it is important to set out the story of risk management; how it began and developed. We then examine efforts to standardize modern practices, which are significantly based on the central idea that we can foresee future risk events and prepare in advance to deal with them. There our analysis will be influenced by what Nassim Taleb refers to as "the teleological fallacy," namely "the illusion that you know exactly where you are going, and that you knew exactly where you were going in the past, and that others have succeeded in the past by knowing where they were going."[30]

What then follows is a look at how actual practices relate to stated guidelines, where through the illustration of various case studies we find that there is a significant space between guidelines and actual practices, which leads us to investigate whether the 'space in between' is telling us something of importance. As a consequence, we arrive at a new way of viewing risk management, which at its heart is based on four propositions:

1. Risk management is more properly understood as 'uncertainty management' (though we stake no claim to that title).
2. Understanding and addressing human nature and perceptions is a fundamental and central function in risk management.
3. The essential nature of risk management is primarily critical thinking in the face of an uncertain world. It is only secondarily a managerial function employing tools, techniques, systems, and processes.
4. Owing to the focus on humans, it is values (individual, organizational, and social) that drive decisions and actions. This emphasis on the morality behind risk management places us in the challenging role of confronting some aspects of human nature including the basic instinct to adopt purely defensive, reactive, fearful positions in response to high levels of uncertainty. Tara Swart and her colleagues state: "Our brain needs a leader to create environments that *feel* safe and certain, even when the world is far from being either."[31] We believe this implies an ostrich reaction—sticking one's head in the sand as opposed to dealing with the real issues—which in our case is to proactively think about (and undertake) ways to deal with uncertainty and the unknowable future.

"When life strips off all her finery, what remains is fortune. Everything that happens is a constant collision of tossed dice." One might despair that the constant collision of tossed dice suggests nothing can be done. We are at the mercy of the Fates. We hope to establish the recognition of truth in Calasso's statement as more of a clarion call, summoning us to reorient our thinking about the nature and purpose of risk management. And as a consequence, we intend to make the argument that important and effective things *can* be done.

NOTES

1 Roberto Calasso (1993). *The Marriage of Cadmus and Harmony*. Vintage Books, New York.
2 The International Organization for Standardization. *ISO 31000:2018 Risk Management: Guidelines*.
3 Nassim Nicholas Taleb (2007). *The Black Swan: The Impact of the Highly Improbable*. Random House, New York.
4 Nassim Nicholas Taleb (2013). *Antifragile: Things that Gain from Disorder*. Penguin Books, London (p. 189).
5 Carlo Rovelli (2018). *The Order of Time*. Allen Lane, Milton Keynes (p. 97).
6 This issue is summarized in Roberto, M.A., Bohmer, R.M.J., and Edmondson, A.C. (2006). Facing ambiguous threats, *Harvard Business Review*, 84(11): 106–113.
7 Some key aspects that touch on the problem with committing to 'the long run' can be found in Weitzner, D. and Darroch, J. (2010). The limits of strategic rationality: Ethics, enterprise risk management and governance, *Journal of Business Ethics*, 92: 361–372.
8 Aspects of the risk management story are found in Smith, D. and Fischbacher, M. (2009). The changing nature of risk and risk management: The challenge of borders, uncertainty and resilience, *Risk Management*, 11(1): 1–12.
9 An excellent review of the current state of affairs is found in Bromiley, P., McShane, M., Nair, A. and Rustambekov, E. (2014). Enterprise risk management: Review, critique, and research directions, *Long Range Planning*, 48(4): 265–276.
10 American Accounting Association (AAA), American Institute of Certified Public Accountants (AICPA), Financial Executives International (FEI), The Institute of Internal Auditors (IIA), and the National Association of Accountants [now the Institute of Management Accountants (IMA)].
11 In collaboration with the Association of Insurance and Risk Manager (AIRMIC) and the Public Risk Management Association (Alarm).
12 For example, the ISO 22301 business continuity management standard, which specifies management systems to protect against disruptive incidents and recover business operations.
13 See, for example, RIMS—The Risk Management Society; PRMIA—The Professional Risk Managers' International Association; GARP—The Global Association of Risk Professionals; PRMA—Public Risk Management Association; and so forth.
14 CAS (Casualty Actuarial Society). *Overview of Enterprise Risk Management*. May 2003 (p. 8).
15 The Institute of Risk Management (IRM). Risk Appetite and Tolerance: Guidance for Practitioners.
16 Prakash A. Shimpi (2002). Integrating risk management and capital management, *Journal of Applied Corporate Finance*, 14(4): 27–40.

17 Paape, L. and Spekle, R.F. (2012). The adoption and design of enterprise risk management practices, *European Accounting Review*, 21(3): 533–564.

18 Andersen, T.J. and Schrøder, P.W. (2010). *Strategic Risk Management Practice: How to Deal Effectively with Major Corporate Exposures*. Cambridge University Press, Cambridge, UK.

19 Aswath Damodaran (2008). *Strategic Risk Taking: A Framework for Risk Management*. Wharton School Publishing, Upper Saddle River, NJ.

20 Power, M. (2009). The risk management of nothing, *Accounting, Organizations and Society*, 34(6–7): 849–855.

21 Miller, K.D. (2009). Organizational risk after modernism, *Organization Studies*, 30(2/3): 157–180.

22 Kantur, D. and Isery-Say, A. (2012). Organizational resilience: A conceptual integrative framework, *Journal of Management & Organization*, 18(6): 762–773.

23 Vogus, T.J. and Sutcliffe, K.M. (2007). Organizational resilience: Towards a theory and research agenda. In International Conference on IEEE Systems, Man and Cybernetics, 2007. ISIC: 3418–3422.

24 Datta, P.P. and Christopher, M.G. (2011). Information sharing and coordination mechanisms for managing uncertainty in supply chains: A simulation study, *International Journal of Production Research*, 49(3): 765–803.

25 Andersen, T.J. and Fredens, K. (2013). The responsive organization. *Center for Global Strategic Responsiveness, CGRS Working Paper Series No. 1, Copenhagen Business School.*

26 Andersen, T.J. (2017). Corporate responsible behavior in multinational enterprise, *International Journal of Organizational Analysis*, 25(3): 485–505.

27 Kinman, B. (2012). Building a risk-resilient organization, *Resilience: A Journal of Strategy and Risk, pwc.*

28 Gino, F. and Staats, B. (2015). Why organizations don't learn, *Harvard Business Review*, 93(11): 110–118.

29 Meyer, R. and Kunreuter, H. (2017). *The Ostrich Paradox: Why We Underprepare for Disasters*, Wharton Business School Press, Philadelphia, PA.

30 Nassim Nicholas Taleb (2013). *Antifragile: Things that Gain from Disorder*. Penguin Books, London. (p. 170).

31 Tara Swart, Kitty Chrisholm and Paul Brown (2015). *Neuroscience for Leadership: Harnessing the Brain Gain Advantage*. Palgrave Macmillan, London. (p. 57).

2 The story of risk management

The opposite of a correct statement is an incorrect statement. The opposite of a profound truth is another profound truth (Niels Bohr). By this, he means that we require a larger reading of the human past, of our relations with each other, the universe and God, a retelling of our older tales to encompass many truths and to let us grow with change.

Neil Postman[1]

Story-telling receives some attention throughout this book. We believe in the power of story-telling, and indeed commit this chapter to an extended story of how the risk management field as we know it today emerged. Postman, as cited above, channels Niels Bohr's emphasis on 'the larger reading' indicating the critical importance of a temperament suited to a wide-ranging view of the things that influence the world, and a sensibility consistent with an open-minded, thoughtful engagement.

Risk managers are frequently reminded that risks and uncertainties do not just exist in the present and the future, but also in the past. Typically, lack of awareness of this fact arises from a failure to understand (or perhaps 'appreciate' is a better word) the past and the unknown; but often it rests within assumptions about the past that provide comfort to and validate our own prejudices and opinions. This chapter ultimately sets forward one of the fundamental issues arising from that past: contingency. We typically assume that present-day outcomes are the result (for good or ill) of some abiding logical philosophy, linearity, or other deterministic drivers, when—in fact—it is the contingency of evolving circumstances that most often rules.

As noted previously, ISO 31000 comes in for some critical analysis in our book, but credit-where-credit-is-due, its emphasis on understanding context as the basis for any effective risk management effort is, well, inspired. We would go so far as to say that exploring and understanding the context should be the most important part of any effort to implement effective risk management.

THE RISK MANAGEMENT STORY

If risk management were to be simply defined as any conscious effort to assess and address the potential consequences of uncertain events, then risk management has been practiced informally since the dawn of time. The way humans acted individually and within social structures bore witness to an awareness of environmental uncertainty and its effects. Prehistoric humans banded together in tribes to conserve resources, share responsibilities, and provide some protection against the uncertainties of daily life. By working together, sharing diverse tasks, cultivating special skills and ideas, and even telling stories, humans were able to address and overcome many of the adverse environmental odds and together persevere by generating more productive ways of dealing with an uncertain environment. Let us add in passing that at many critical moments the human race was just lucky.

Even today, this *informal* or *instinctive* risk management is practiced by everyone, including—notably here—the individuals that execute their daily business activities inside our organizations. We 'measure twice and cut once' to avoid failures, we look both ways before crossing a busy street to reduce the likelihood of serious injury, and we exercise and eat a proper diet to improve our prospects for good health—in other words, we rely on common sense. Hence, humans have long toiled under the implicit thesis that competent humans and social groups manage risks and uncertainty effectively, even in instances where they obviously do not consider their efforts to be *per se* risk management.

More recently, history has shown institutions and organizations adopting 'informally formal' approaches to risk management, often informed by the organization's culture and values. Indeed, we see organizations practicing informal risk management up to and including today. This is to be applauded because it suggests that organizations have internalized the necessity to be consciously aware of risk and uncertainty. The problem with only internalizing risk awareness is that many sources of risk and uncertainty are highly complex, confusing, and difficult to understand. Plus, as we will see, human perception itself is a source of risk and uncertainty. So, conscious application does seem necessary too.

Having noted the informal side of risk management, let us be clear as we move on. This book is focused on *formal* practices undertaken by social structures—firms, organizations, and public institutions. In these contexts, the history of formal, self-consciously aware risk management practices is of much shorter duration and limited scope.

We begin

To provide just a touchstone as we begin our story, let us restate and clarify our view of risk, uncertainty, and unknowability in relation to one another.

Risk, uncertainty, unknowability

<u>Risk</u>: when expected outcomes of future events, positive or negative, can be predicted on the basis of the distribution of comparable previous events

<u>Uncertainty</u>: when expected outcomes of future events, positive or negative cannot be predicted because events are unique, irregular, and abrupt/sudden

<u>Unknowability</u>: things will happen that cannot be foreseen (*unknown unknowns*), positive or negative, and complex dynamic systems can lead to unexpected outcomes

---

Business historians have found that many early 20th-century organizational activities anticipated the emergence of risk management (workplace safety being an obvious example).[2] Nevertheless, formal risk management is essentially a post–World War II phenomenon as is the case of other areas within the wider field of management studies and practice. Even within this limited time frame, risk management practices adopted in most organizations prior to 1960 were extremely narrow in scope.

The early years: 1945–1970

Embedded among the multitude of social, economic, political, and technical/scientific responses and efforts employed to recover from the destruction wrought by World War II we find an expansion and sophistication of management science, education, and training. For example, during this period business schools, professional communities, and scientifically oriented management academies began to proliferate.

There are specific reasons for this, but notably this development occurred in some part to capture and advance the managerial and administrative learning experiences that arose from the prosecution of a global war and the efforts thereafter to rebuild modern societies through commercial enterprise and public initiatives. To be sure, other factors played a role: the labor market impacts of returning veterans, the resumption of earlier business practice research, and policy initiatives to rebuild especially Europe and Asia and establish a global economic order.

There is some small controversy as to whether scholars accelerated the development of risk management as a concept during this period, or whether businesses and consultancies advanced practices which subsequently inspired the scholars. There is a stronger case for the latter view in all aspects of management science. However, there is now little doubt that the period from roughly 1955 to 1964 gave birth to the conceptualization of *formal* risk management practices, both academically and professionally.[3]

As with most modern managerial functions, risk management did not spring to life fully formed. Without question the earliest and most influential manifestation was *insurance-buying*. Many current risk management positions evolved out of the insurance-buying function and as such insurance-buying proves to be a historical artifact that casts a very long shadow; notably by the way we often interpret a risk as something that only, or primarily, represents a threatening loss potential. This influence extends to the academic field of risk management. The science of risk management often evolved within insurance studies programs at colleges, universities, and technical schools and many of the preeminent centers of risk management studies have continued this traditional association. Tellingly, a preeminent academic journal in the field today, the *Journal of Risk and Insurance*, was known as the *Journal of Insurance* until 1964.

In the early days most organizations that practiced any formal risk or insurance management had a part-time, or full-time insurance buyer employed whose duties essentially covered the placement and management of the insurance portfolio and some related tasks. Managing effectively in the global insurance and re-insurance markets requires professional skills, insights, and experience with the engagement of trained employees. Over time, within a number of organizations the duties of the insurance buyer began to expand into ancillary areas (e.g., application of risk audits and risk control activities) as the number and types of insurance covers multiplied and the issues associated with insurance exposures became more complex. Sometimes the behavior or requirements of insurers in the market influenced this expansion, sometimes it was the initiative or ability of individual managers, and sometimes the growth was caused by the specific risk characteristics of the organization. Nevertheless, the expansion of the function was sufficiently noticeable by the mid-1950s for both academicians and practitioners to begin the process of defining this specific managerial function as risk management. Among many notable developments, the first textbooks on the subject of risk management began appearing by the early 1960s.

Importantly, in our view, by 1960 the risk management field had already been locked into a core assumption about its orientation. It was primarily engaged in identifying and addressing potential *threats* to avoid suffering the impacts of fortuitous losses. The idea that risk also might be a source of *opportunities* to be exploited was not much part of the early vocabulary. Adjunct to this was an important assumption, which was fully the result of the centrality of insurance to early risk management practices. In order for insurance to function, there must be a reasonable degree of measurability of the frequency and magnitude of negative outcomes, so it necessarily became the case that the focus was on risks—what, in the 1920s economist Frank Knight referred to as measurable uncertainty.[4] Logically, for this obvious reason the function became known as *risk* management rather than, say, *uncertainty* management.

The emphasis on risk was clearly an advantage in the sense that to the uninformed observer everything that happens is uncertain or unknowable, whereas a discipline associated with observing, measuring, and statistically assessing the potential consequences of risk events serves to advance better risk management capabilities with respect to those risks. And, as noted, it also goes a long way in explaining why the focus on measurable uncertainty remains a cornerstone of risk management today.[5] We tend to deal with the things we can measure, whereas it is easier to ignore those things that cannot be measured, even though they might be some of the most important factors an organization or firm encounters.

The influence of the historical roots in insurance had other impacts as well. Perhaps most notably, risk management was—as a practical matter—associated with financial management and was almost invariably seen as an activity carried out within an organization's finance function. However, by the 1960s, a number of risk managers (the title risk manager—no surprise—became more widely used during this period) expressed the view that their duties were beginning to move beyond the realm of merely financial activities or insurance-buying. As a bit of marginalia, it is a virtual article of faith in the risk management profession that in 1963 Doug Barlow of Massey Ferguson became the first individual to be given the official title of Risk Manager.

The 'middle ages': 1970–2005

By the late 1960s one of the more important evolutionary developments in the risk management field was a decided movement away from a sole reliance on traditional insurance products. Although insurance continued to be widely used as an effective risk transfer tool, change was afoot in larger organizations. Many risk managers discovered that insurance covers did not always meet the specific organizational needs or provide the least expensive solution. Additionally, the adoption of new management techniques such as safety engineering, loss reduction measures, and—later on—total quality management and continuous improvement, could contain the impact of risk and uncertainty on many organizational processes.

Further, some of the largest organizations found that they were able to forecast certain types of losses as well as the professional insurers, and had a sufficiently large diversified portfolio of exposures that made it beneficial to consider retaining or self-insuring those risks. In other organizations, other types of loss prevention and risk mitigation activities were found to be an effective way to respond to particularly challenging exposures; actions that often led to significant reductions in reliance on commercial insurance.

While this was occurring the finite capacity of the insurance industry yielded up periodic insurance availability and affordability crises due to cyclical loss experience and changes in competitive market intensity. This push-pull effect accelerated both a broadening of the insurance buyer/ risk manager function alongside a relative de-emphasis or downscaling of insurance buying activities as the predominant risk management focus.

Although insurance buying clearly laid the foundation for the risk management field, and continues to be a key aspect of risk management today, other influences also became important during that time period. The formation of professional associations like the American Society of Insurance Management (which, tellingly, later became the Risk and Insurance Management Society, and today is called the Risk Management Society or RIMS for short) helped crystalize an early framework incorporating a wider-ranging view of risk management. The risk management structure proposed by RIMS set forward a rational approach to assess potential risk events and introduce measures to reduce, hedge, insure, or otherwise proactively deal with those exposures.

The elements of the proposed approach were expressed in the following sequential elements of a formalized risk management function:

1. **Goal identification**. The alignment of risk management goals and objectives where fulfillment of the objectives of the organization is seen as a fundamental task of the risk manager. This part of the risk management process identifies the relationship between risk management and the objectives of the organization.

2. **Risk assessment**. Risk assessment consists of three related activities. First, risks and uncertainties that affect the organization must be *identified*. Identification of risks is usually accompanied by both *hazard identification* and *exposure identification*. Hazards are activities or conditions that create, or increase the likelihood of loss or the loss amount.

   Identification is followed by *analysis*. It is not sufficient to know that hazards and exposures to loss exist. The risk manager must understand the nature of those hazards and their exposures, how they come to exist, and how they interact to produce a loss. Perceptions of risk, as well as uncertainty, were subject to some attention too.

   Analysis is related to the final assessment activity, *risk measurement*. Risk measurement evaluates the likelihood of loss and the value of loss along the dimensions of frequency and severity. The measurement process may take the form of a qualitative assessment— this loss is pretty likely to occur—or a more sophisticated numerical estimation process.

3. **Risk control**. Risk control activities are those that focus upon avoiding, preventing, reducing, or otherwise controlling risks and uncertainties. Risk control activities can take simple forms, such as making sure that a restaurant kitchen has functioning fire extinguishers. They can also be complex, such as developing a catastrophe contingency plan to use in a potential emergency situation.

4. **Risk financing**. Risk financing activities provide the means of reimbursing losses that occur and for funding other programs to reduce the effects of uncertainty and risk. Normally, some losses will occur despite the risk control efforts. The financing of these losses can include measures such as the purchase of insurance coverage, the establishment of alternative risk financing tools, the use of letters of credit, etc.

In later years risk control and risk financing have often been collapsed into the terms risk treatment or risk response.

5. **Program administration.** This component establishes procedures followed in the day-to-day operations of the risk management function. For example, procedures for buying insurance, or the structuring of the program review and evaluation process fall into program administration. Procedures for communicating program efforts and results to intended target audiences are another example. Also, program administration is determined in the context of the specific organization and its resources. The task requires detailed knowledge about how the organization operates, its goals and objectives, its history, its people, and capabilities.

This is not really a complicated framework and indeed its simplicity allowed for general managerial applications outside of traditional 'insurable risk' settings. Thus, for example, the concepts and principles of early risk management were applied to workplace safety efforts and employee benefits management, facility security initiatives, post M&A integration, and communications security methods—to cite just a few examples.

In the late 1970s the previously mentioned operations management theories and practices began to expand and extend their influence. While important in their own right, they ran parallel with corresponding movement in the risk management field. Total quality management (TQM), continuous improvement (CI), and zero defects (ZD) practices introduced a more scrupulous investigation of operating procedures focusing on the handling of defects, errors, and unusual outcomes, while delving more deeply into the underlying causes of those incidents.[6]

Operations and risk management never fully merged but there was considerable cross-pollinization of thinking and applications. Perhaps notably from a risk management standpoint, TQM, CI, and ZD pulled risk management thinking well outside the realm of insurable risks and really introduced the idea that there were many applications of risk management that might lead to more effective approaches integrating a wider range of risk management efforts. It remains important to point out that all of these developments still emphasized that risk management was engaged in threat-management, and that the challenge remained focused on measurable uncertainty.

Financial risk management: a key development

One of the most influential stories in the expansion of the scope of risk management, undoubtedly, is the emergence of *financial risk management*. Financial risk management is a form of risk management that principally arose from the financial services sector as a systematic approach to dealing with specific types of financial risks such as credit risks, foreign exchange risks, interest rate risks, commodity price risks, and investment market risks. Although financial institutions had faced these risks for centuries, in the early 1970s the financial sector experienced some dramatic and hence influential crisis events. In the United States, as just one example, mutual savings banks had thrived for years providing secured long-term fixed rate housing loans to customers funded by stable deposits from low-rate savings accounts. The high-inflation environment of that era changed this formula as the increasing interest expenses on the mutuals' liabilities squeezed profitability and eventually threatened institutional survival.

More broadly, for decades the US regulatory setup (brought into law in response to the Great Crash of 1929 and ensuing Great Depression) banned banks from operating across interstate borders, which encouraged major money center banks such as Citibank, Chase Manhattan Bank, and JPMorgan to expand their international banking activities. The increasing internationalization of corporate business activities propelled that development further as the global networks of large international banks sought to follow and serve their multinational corporate customers. This, combined with increasingly volatile foreign exchange markets after the abolishment of gold-linked currency parities in the early 1970s, soon revealed that international banks and multinational corporations had to manage their sizeable foreign exchange exposures. The increase in exposures to foreign exchange rate risks also occurred at a time of higher commodity price volatility, precipitated in part by the oil price hikes after the Organization of Petroleum Exporting Countries restricted the production of oil in the early 1970s to boost their own revenues.

All of these developments prompted financial institutions and multinational corporations to consider adopting more formal measures to address such financial risks and ultimately to develop financial instruments to manage the underlying exposures and to exchange them in open international over-the-counter markets. An early result produced something of a circular effect between the academy and the business world; academicians began to study the phenomenon of financial risk management, and their output fed back into the business world where new theories and ideas were applied.

This new academic thinking focused on multinational financial management, which led to the introduction of distinct business school courses[7] and research into more esoteric financial topics related to the pricing and management of so-called *derivative* contracts. New options pricing methodologies, such as the famous Black-Scholes option pricing model,[8] became a major impetus to one particularly broad research stream focused on investment applications of derivative contracts. This growing interest ultimately inspired the distinct and highly quantitative academic field of financial risk management.

On the practitioner side, it is interesting to note that the Chicago Board of Trade was an important and early launching pad for the emergence of many of these exchange-traded financial risk instruments, where different forward/futures contracts—explained below—were introduced to hedge exposures to, not precisely financial institution risks, but rather to buyer/seller exposure to commodity price volatility.[9] The location in the US-Midwest was obviously not a coincidence as it is there that is found a large agricultural hinterland producing essential farm products like wheat, corn, soybeans, cattle, hogs, and dairy presenting many natural sellers (farmers) and buyers (food processors) as the basis for active markets in agricultural contracts. Since their emergence in the 1970s, these contracts have been extended to also cover various financial risks with weather risks and catastrophe risks being only two notable risk management-focused extensions in application. In addition to the simpler futures contracts, other contracts reveal a more exotic cast, such as options, spread-options, and swaps—again, all collectively falling under the general appellation of *derivatives*.

Briefly a derivative is a financial contract whose value depends on the value of one or more underlying assets, or indices of asset values. In the context of financial risk management, these instruments are essentially a hedging arrangement that allows buyers and sellers of the contracts to reduce—or modify—their exposure to the financial volatility arising from a position in the underlying asset—be that related to commodity prices, foreign exchange rates, interest rates, or equity prices. However, one key distinction is that these financial risk management tools differ from traditional risk financing tools like insurance in their potential use for *risk speculation* (that is, *increasing* the exposures). What is more, since these instruments are derivatives, the positions can be established without investing fully in the underlying assets and thereby become potential vehicles to create levered positions for relatively smaller amounts of invested capital.

Development of these tools through the 1980s, 1990s, and 2000s also introduced a high degree of complexity and sophisticated challenges for top managers. These risk management instruments could themselves be considered a potential source of risk/uncertainty for organizational managers that did not fully comprehend or understand the eventual exposures they created for themselves. The bankruptcy of Orange County in California in 1996 due to excessive investments in risky interest rate derivatives was an early warning alarm in this regard, but many other examples of this kind can be found.

In the late 1980s JPMorgan developed a so-called value-at-risk (VaR) system allowing risk managers to assess the overall exposures of engaging in many financial instruments whose price fluctuations could be more or less correlated. This system was seen to provide a better and more 'holistic' overview of the many financial exposures encountered by a large global bank. It arguably reflected a general trend to consider the interrelationships between different risks and consider the aggregate effects on the total corporate exposure.

The VaR methodology provided a single metric calculated within a certain level of confidence, say a likelihood of 95% or 99% that the aggregated loss for a single trading day (week or month) would not increase beyond a certain absolute level. Provided this number was a reasonably accurate prediction of future market conditions, it would allow the banks to determine whether their total trading and/or investment risks were reasonably within the capacity of their capital reserves. Ultimately, many corporate non-financial enterprises began to apply the same principles to assess the aggregate riskiness of their business portfolios, which had particular relevance for energy companies and other users of global commodities. These developments further solidified in the minds of many that risk management was primarily a financial management matter where almost any type of exposure could be quantified, calculated, monitored, and controlled through sophisticated technical means.

Finally, as a clinical note here, the common applications of the VaR models relied on normally distributed financial return data, which turns out not to hold in case of extreme market events. An additional weakness was the method's reliance on positive risk diversification effects from less than perfectly correlated returns. Hence, in a crisis situation a dynamic complex system like globally interconnected financial markets can lead to unexpected extreme outcomes in the asset prices, which are— undoubtedly—problematic. This is exactly what happened during the financial crisis in 2008. Without digressing into minute technicalities, we believe that the general trust in common financial risk management practices among financial institutions made many large international banks take on exposures linked to the US subprime loan market— exposures that dramatically exceeded what they believed they had on their books.

The enterprise risk management concept: a key inflection point

Looking back on the historical evolution of risk management, it might be said that the story shows the emergence of a number of *technical risk management* functions, first led by insurance-buying techniques and subsequently more sophisticated financial risk management methodologies, but also including affiliated managerial developments dealing with operational exposures such as health and safety, IT security, product quality, general security, supply chain disruptions, and other risks. This development expanded the reach of risk managers into overlapping practice areas and ultimately revealed to both practitioners and academics the possibilities of an increasingly integrative view of organization-wide risk management.[10]

Related to the integrating dynamic although of a more technical nature, the Bank for International Settlements (BIS) initiated a requirement that banks measure and manage their 'operational risks' in addition to the more conventional financial risks. The enormous traffic of financial transactions cleared and settled across many multinational financial institutions each and every day around the globe represent significant exposures, as human errors, systems flaws, and IT breakdowns were seen to have large and powerfully threatening consequences. An almost immediately observable issue here was the challenge of quantifying these types of exposures, and identifying the key factors within and across organizations that required ongoing monitoring. It is fair to say that this turned out to be a hard nut to crack—but not for lack of trying.

Until the Basel II reforms were released by the BIS during 2004–2006,[11] operational risk was simply considered a residual business outcome that was difficult, or impossible to manage—an unavoidable cost of doing banking. However, we think it significant that the Basel II Committee considered operational exposures as potential losses from failed internal processes and systems and prescribed new standards for banks to manage. The Committee also promoted the collection of data on historical operational losses to model the exposures and calculate capital reserves to cover potential future losses. Thus, from a somewhat different direction, the idea of looking at risks in a more comprehensive and integrated way began to take hold.

Integrative ideas and practices emerge

We think it safe to say that by the 1990s the risk management field had entered a phase where two parallel developments were occurring. On the academic side scholars continued a search for a unifying theory or idea of risk management, and on the practitioner side an argument began to win adherents that significant value could be derived from better coordination across the various technical tasks and practices.

For scholars, the seeming solution was found in modern finance theory, where risk management practices were demonstrated (although not conclusively from empirical studies, but from conceptual arguments) to increase shareholder value.[12] Hence, a corporate finance perspective on risk management practices would see this as a way to impose properly determined risk-return requirements on risky business projects. This, in turn, would lead to better prioritizations of investment decisions where expected returns could be attained within acceptable risk parameters. The result would be that managers proposing new projects in different parts of the organization would account for all the major risk factors in the investment proposals by ensuring a proper risk-adjusted return on the committed capital. The risk management function could assist them in evaluating and reviewing the risk-return trade-offs.

This approach proposes a dual emphasis on day-to-day risk decisions made in the operating entities as well as the reporting of aggregate corporate exposures to the executive team and higher governance levels. It means that the risk management function serves corporate governance by helping to determine a proper level of acceptable risk at the enterprise level; information contained in a so-called *risk appetite statement*. That is, the enterprise risk management practices conducted by the corporate risk office would identify, assess, and aggregate all the major business risks as a useful way to monitor and manage the total corporate exposures within reasonable thresholds and limits.[13]

On the practitioner side, the risk management process is somewhat less easy to summarize as there was a significant degree of difference across firms and organizations. Early developments seemed to suggest that a wider-ranging approach to risk management would likely need to be consistent with the organizational structure and cultural traits and therefore would need to be possibly quite differently tailored depending on the context of the individual organization. Having noted that, generalized ideas began to emerge regarding so-called 'integrated risk management' (a transitional label that was seen in the run-up to the eventual introduction of the ERM concept). Through experimentation and the promotion of the concept interest grew noticeably among practitioners.

The result of the academic and practitioner activities was a widening exploration of ways to justify the integration of technical practices and to find and implement more holistic and consistent approaches to assessing and addressing the major risks and exposures of corporations and institutions in general. Owing to the specific progression of this interest, the emerging integrated organization-wide risk management perspective came to be viewed mainly as the additive result of linking the various technical risk management efforts together. In other words, the risk management function came to be seen as a very large, but still technical, risk management exercise.

It is important to note that two weaknesses of this emergent view were evident very early on. One was the challenge of determining how the process of integrating risk management would actually occur in an organization, and another was the question of how to ensure that all the key risks truly were being assessed and addressed. Entwined in both issues was the particularly vexing question of who performed the integrating, organizing, and linking that is necessary to make this holistic integrated risk management approach work. A third issue gradually emerged along the way to challenge integration efforts; namely whether all the different specialized risk areas really needed to be fully integrated, or if there is a case to be made for keeping some of these efforts separate so they could operate independently within their specific area of expertise.

Knowledgeable observers began to respond to these—and other—issues and the emerging solution to the challenges of integrated risk management eventually became folded under the title of enterprise risk management (ERM), which was further elaborated by a number of standardized risk management frameworks. As noted in the previous chapter, maybe the most influential framework—at least in the US—originates from the Committee of Sponsoring Organizations of the Treadway Commission (COSO). COSO produced numerous other statements on financial matters, but it was the occurrence of major corporate failures including companies like Enron, Tyco International, and WorldCom in the early 2000s that got COSO into the risk management business. The legislative response to these corporate failures was the Sarbanes-Oxley Act in 2002. Prompted by (or at least coincident with) Sarbanes-Oxley, COSO engaged PwC to develop a risk management framework, which was published as the *Enterprise Risk Management—Integrated Framework* in 2004.

Similar developments happened elsewhere in the world. A notable (and earlier) development was the first Australian–New Zealand standard, AS/NZS 4360 *Risk Management* published in 1995. A UK-based *Risk Management Standard* was issued in 2002 by three main risk organizations, the Institute of Risk Management (IRM), the National Forum for Risk Management in the Public Sector (ALARM), and the Association of Insurance and Risk Managers (AIRMIC). This framework was subsequently adopted by the European Federation of Risk Management Associations (FERMA). The basic principles of AS/ NZS 4360, IRM, ALARM, AIRMIC, and FERMA have since been incorporated and extended in the ISO 31000 guidance, which was published in 2009.

The COSO framework defined ERM as:

> [a] process, effected by an entity's board of directors, management and other personnel, applied in strategy-setting and across the enterprise, designed to identify potential events that may affect the entity, and manage risks to be within its risk appetite, to provide reasonable assurance regarding the achievement of entity objectives.

In other words, it captures a high-level governance approach whose success depends on the ability to satisfy predetermined strategic objectives within specified risk limits signed off by the board of directors. More will be said about COSO, but it is clear that the ERM idea not only aspired to integrate existing technical risk management functions but also added new ones such as risk governance and strategic leadership concerns. This signified an overarching aim of addressing the issue of how enterprise-wide risk management practices ideally should be planned, implemented, and managed.[14]

Modern risk management: post-2005

In subsequent years the ERM movement gained traction and continued to dominate thinking and practice, extending into the current day.[15] Virtually every developed country in the world now has some form of requirement or legal expectation for risk management to be practiced in this way. Just to offer a few illustrations, the OECD Principles of Corporate Governance originally developed in 1999, updated in 2004, and then later in 2015 highlighted the need to report on reasonably foreseeable and material risks to give market participants important financial information. However, it stopped short of giving specific recommendations, merely suggesting that risk updates should be as detailed as needed to inform investors.

The German Accounting Standards Board issued an accounting standard on the reporting of risks (GAS-5) in 2000 requiring that material risks be described in the management reports. The European Union (EU) addressed mandatory risk reporting in the Accounts Modernization and Transparency directives 2004–2005 that promoted risk disclosure in annual reports with information on principal risks and half-yearly management reports on how they were being addressed. That is, EU-based companies were required to provide information on financial risks and in addition explain their corporate risk profile— including strategic and operational exposures.

EU policy requirements on audit committees and their roles to secure proper internal controls and risk management processes were considered in a new Company Law directive from 2006 requiring audit committees to monitor internal controls, audits, and risk management systems.[16] To support the implementation, positions were solicited from professional communities including FERMA, who emphasized (to no big surprise) an integrated holistic approach with internal controls coordinated by a central risk management function.[17]

In a joint guidance paper with the European Confederation of Institutes of Internal Auditing (ECIIA) FERMA promoted the so-called three lines of defense model based on the principles of ERM and emphasizing operational risk management, risk governance reporting, and independent auditing of processes.[18] The ECIIA ascribed the 2008 financial crisis to the absence of adequate warning signs given to executives and their boards calling for improved governance, risk management, and internal control processes. A later update touted a top-down-driven board approved strategy formulation where ERM should ensure that intended goals are achieved and expected returns maximized within predetermined risk limits, or in line with the stated *risk appetite*.[19] This ERM-driven three lines of defense model heeding operational risk support, corporate risk governance reporting, and independent retrospective audits is also considered a consistent and integral part of the COSO risk management framework.[20]

The ERM three lines of defense model has been widely promoted by financial regulators and academics referring to a wide consensus claiming that substantial governance failures contributed to the 2008 financial crisis and therefore calling for stricter board-level procedures with legally binding rules.[21] Hence, the Basel Committee on Banking Supervision (BCBS) issued corporate governance guidelines in 2015 emphasizing risk procedures and calling for an independent risk management function headed by a Chief Risk Officer (CRO).

The OECD similarly promoted CRO positions in the banking sector as did the European Commission. In short, the ERM framework was further emphasized as *the* appropriate way to manage risks and secure proper risk governance while instituting an independent risk management function headed by a CRO. The title of CRO was not really a new invention; it had existed in (particularly US-based) corporations for some time, but the policy-makers and their influencers effectively introduced a new class of risk managers to deal with corporate risks in accordance with ERM.

To add some substance to these developments, the Basel Committee's guidelines on corporate governance for banks[22] established that an effective risk management function should be directed by a CRO with sufficient stature, independence, resources, and board access to accomplish a number of key activities: identify material risks, assess them to determine bank exposure, implement the enterprise-wide risk governance framework including *risk culture* and *risk appetite*, monitor risk-taking activities within the approved risk appetite, establish early warning triggers, challenge decisions giving rise to material risk, and report to senior management, the board, and the risk committee on all of these items. This follows the known principles of the ERM framework. There obviously is more vocabulary to support this 'to do' list, but the BIS was still not very explicit in defining what for example *sufficient stature*, *risk culture*, and *risk appetite* mean in a risk practice managed across a large social structure with individual actors.

SOME REFLECTIONS ON THE STORY

Well, that is our story—at least it brings us to the present day. Chapters 3 and 4 will delve into a more structured analysis of the current scene, but it does seem appropriate to tee-up some of the key issues that are suggested by the preceding story.

First, despite the seemingly triumphant tale of emerging ERM domination there have been voices of concern expressed about the consequences of the acceptance of ERM as the ideal, fully validated approach to risk management. Professor Michael Power of the London School of Economics[23] for example has warned that blind adherence to formal rule-based processes like ERM, with a prime emphasis on auditable trails of documentation, may deprive organizations of the ability to use professional judgment in their ongoing business decisions. The formalized procedures and practices might eventually trump conscious thinking about the specific conditions around emergent decision situations. He also argued that ERM is flawed by design because it is unable to comprehend and articulate the critical risks formed by uncertain future events and emergent risk scenarios that are hard to quantify.[24]

A second challenge arises from a few recognized studies of the 2008 financial crisis, which provided some sobering insights about the governance conditions before the crisis struck. In a comprehensive study,

Beltratti and Stulz[25] found that banks with shareholder-friendly boards were those that performed worst during the crisis, where those banks that posted the highest returns in 2006 also fared the worst during the crisis. So, the issue did not appear to be inadequate risk governance, but rather seemed linked to flawed board behavior and lack of good judgment that pushed these banks into maximizing shareholder wealth and accepting excessive exposures to achieve that—which eventually led to dramatic unexpected losses when the markets fell.

Also emerging from the research, it was found that while ERM promises a holistic approach framed as a rational fully informed decision-making process, actually making that happen was challenging. For example, in reality this approach proved to have strong signs of being heavily influenced by psychological flaws and cognitive biases among key decision-makers.[26] Illustrative of those flaws and biases is evidence that individuals often tend to underestimate the potential effects of uncertain future events. And to the extent powerful individuals have greater confidence in their own judgments, they are also likely to misperceive the potential effects of uncertainty even more. This seems to be an essential insight from events under the financial crisis, but one that has not yet been fully acknowledged. The bigger irony is that the observed urge to impose stricter formal risk governance requirements does not guarantee that the judgments made by decision-makers up to and during a crisis are any less biased than before. In fact, the opposite could very well be the case.

As the story of ERM suggests, the frameworks are largely produced and refined by accountants, auditors, controllers, and people within the economics and finance professions. Consequently, that framework tends to be based on theories about optimal conditions for achieving desired outcomes such as profits and risk adjusted market returns. They typically propose methods and tools intended to reach the optimal outcomes under the assumed conditions but tend to disregard the potential intervening influences of organizational behaviors, the psychology of social processes, and various human cognitive biases in judgment.[27]

One would think that a more effective method also might require some understanding of different organizational actors, their motivations, and behavioral traits. ERM assumes that all strategic decisions derive from a rational strategic planning process whereas the strategy field for long has realized that some of the most important and influential strategic decisions can, and possibly must, originate from informal processes deep inside the organization beyond the views of executives and board members.

To conclude these comments, note that the remnants of the 2008 financial crisis provided scattered insights that could teach us some useful lessons. Whereas it can be argued that the theoretical assumptions for some of the exposure measures such as the VaR system cannot be fully supported, the crisis was not really the result of serious measurement errors and methodological flaws. While the idea that such misreporting and failure of modeling caused the crisis is a common or convenient belief, it is factually wrong. The crisis was primarily grounded in bad judgments of senior decision-makers that thought they were acting in the best interest of the shareholders to secure maximum returns, while they also—let us be honest—in some cases scored high personal gains along the way. So, the story uncovers the significant influence of judgmental biases and the importance of integrity and morality among key decision-makers acting in the role of custodians for all stakeholders and society more broadly.

In a survey among experienced risk managers in the London market after the 2008 financial crisis, the respondents argued that the banking crisis was not caused by technical risk management failures as much as by failed organizational culture and flawed ethics.[28] In the wake of the 2008 financial crisis, we also note a more modest, somewhat toned down belief in market self-governance with a gradual move by the BIS toward more realistic approaches to quantify operational risk. Expecting higher sophistication among larger banks, those banks were allowed to quantify their operational exposures based on internal model estimates, but the 'relative infancy of the field ... at the time' caused a lack of comparability across the range of internal modelling practices applied by different banks. As a result, the BIS Committee withdrew its recommendation for internal modeling in 2016. Basel III was intended to review the problems in modeling and to issue a restatement between 2013–2015, but that is now delayed until after 2019.

An update on risk management 'standardization'

COSO and ISO 31000 have already been introduced and have been a subject of some discussion. Here we might have chosen to first look at the original 2004 COSO and 2009 ISO 31000 statements, but it is perhaps more focused and appropriate to access COSO's and ISO's most current ideas as expressed in their recent updates. In our view, it is more illuminating to focus on the updates as they not only spell out specific changes from the 2004 and 2009 statements. They also shed light on the issues and limitations embedded in the original documents.[29]

The COSO 2016 update, *Enterprise Risk Management—Aligning Risk with Strategy and Performance*, summarizes its changes as follows:

- Provide greater insight into the role of enterprise risk management when setting and executing strategy.
- Enhance alignment between performance and enterprise risk management.
- Accommodate expectations for governance and oversight.
- Recognize the globalization of markets and operations and the need to apply a common, albeit tailored, approach across geographies.
- Present new ways to view risk in order to set and achieve objectives in the context of greater business complexity.
- Expand reporting to address expectations for greater stakeholder transparency.
- Accommodate evolving technologies and the growth of data analytics in supporting decision-making.

At the risk of offering a slight provocation, it could be said that these changes indicate that the 2004 statement had not positioned ERM as an *input* to strategy formulation, had not fully considered the pursuit of *opportunities* as part of the risk management remit, had not adequately reflected the *governance* and *leadership* dimensions of ERM, and had not fully anticipated the demands made by *globalization*, *stakeholders*, and increasing *complexity*. However, *human behavior* still does not seem to be given the prominent positioning that we see as essential. That said, COSO obviously should be applauded that learning and experiential insights appear to have led to adaptations.

So, COSO is striving to alter its course, and in many respects the recommended changes align with our views. We would be far too harsh to judge COSO on the problems inherent in the 2004 statement; the organization was launching itself into uncharted waters. However, we remain somewhat unsettled about the continued influence of residues from the 2004 statement. That original document now serves as a chapter in our story, and the path-dependency factor leads us to wonder whether fully breaking free from original assumptions and judgments is possible. For example, a recent case study of ERM implementation in a large global organization notes that: "Risk Management had become something between a *fata morgana* and a very expensive folder hidden at the executive office."[30] The concluding experience was expressed quite succinctly in the following quote: "The sad story is that the risk information people collected never really was used or integrated in day-to-day management." This obviously serves to illustrate how difficult it is to turn a codified set of risk management practices into useful applications in a large complex organization populated by many, and diverse, individuals.

Somewhat parallel to the COSO story is the slightly later emergence of the ISO 31000 framework in 2009. Although it is very difficult to set out the relationship between COSO and ISO 31000, as noted previously ISO derives from earlier developments of risk management standards in Australia, New Zealand, and the UK, which over time spread across Europe as something of a 'parallel' initiative to COSO (but also gaining further traction in the wake of the 2008 financial crisis). COSO had only really begun to take hold by 2007–2008, so it cannot really be said that failures within the financial system seen at that time were the result of weaknesses or limitations in the COSO idea. Nevertheless, it is possible to say that some of the issues identified in the recent COSO update were evident very early on (where 'high complexity' and 'overriding focus on systems, controls, and processes' were common concerns).

In any event, ISO undertook the development of guidelines for risk management, which led to its 2009 statement. One of the early compare-and-contrast issues that came to light was the differing philosophies of the two guidance frameworks. It is only simplifying things slightly to argue that COSO tends toward a *rules-based* approach while ISO 31000 represents more of a *principles-based* philosophy. What is interesting to note is that the two updates (COSO, 2016; ISO, 2018) seem to be converging, reflecting—one can imagine—concerns that a rules-based approach tends to lead to box-ticking exercises, whereas a principles-based approach tends to leave managers bewildered as to 'where to begin.'

Still, it is possible to say that the 2018 revision of ISO 31000 retains a principles-based flavor. The guidance emphasizes three elements: principles, framework, and process.

The stated principles of ISO 31000 (2018) are:

Value Creation and Protection through...
- Continual improvement
- Integration
- Structure and comprehensive analyses
- Customized processes
- Inclusive processes
- Dynamic processes
- Use of the best available information
- Considering human and cultural factors.

The ISO 31000 framework consists of Leadership and Commitment that are intended to produce a process of Design, Implementation, Evaluation, Improvement, and Integration. The process can be summarized as:

- Communication and Consultation, leading to ...
- Selection of Scope, Context, Criteria, which direct ...
- Risk Assessment (risk identification, analysis, evaluation), which informs ...
- Risk Treatment, all of which is ...
- Recorded and Reported, which informs ...
- Monitoring and Reviewing.

Perhaps the most interesting addition to ISO 31000 is an explicit acknowledgement of the guideline's relationship to a separate ISO document—called the Annex SL (a guide to management systems standards). Note that neither ISO 31000 nor COSO currently aligns with Annex SL.

Annex SL creates a framework for larger management systems including guidance on scope and design elements as well as control and development elements. Notably, several other ISO guidance standards have been converted to the Annex SL (ISO 9001, ISO 14001, ISO 45001, to name a few). With the inclusion of the Annex SL reference point, ISO 31000 has—in effect—stepped outside itself and is suggesting a development and performance relationship within all large management system processes and projects thus bringing it closer to a status of a codified standard.

It is important to note here that, as with COSO (2016), ISO 31000 (2018) reflects changes to its original document. The most notable changes emphasize the following:

- The principles of risk management have been reviewed, as these are the key criteria for successful risk management.
- The importance of leadership by top management is highlighted, as is the integration of risk management, starting with the governance of the organization.
- Greater emphasis is placed on the iterative nature of risk management, because new knowledge and analysis leads to revision of processes, actions, and controls.
- The content is streamlined with greater focus on sustaining an open systems model to fit multiple needs and contexts.

Using the same 'looking-glass' analysis applied previously to COSO, it seems that the revised ISO also is responding to feedback and perceived limitations including a need to provide greater emphasis on *leadership*, a need to better articulate a somewhat *sharper vision of techniques* (the functional detail), an emphasis on the 'organization-wide' *nature of ERM*, and the *nature of the system* itself.

A short commentary on COSO and ISO

Some of the practitioner learnings from the 2008 financial crisis were that the governance and internal control systems depend heavily on the organizational climate in which they are enacted and that 'risk culture' and ethics somehow need to be at the top of the agenda both in the board rooms as well as among the central regulators. The revised ERM frameworks have taken some note of that, like many of the regulatory bodies, although none of them yet entirely comprehend what this implies for concrete practices or indeed how this can be handled through implementation of formal processes and controls.

There is an urge, it seems, to impose even more formal controls in the belief that this will do the trick for us. But, it will not. We believe (and will argue later) it gives us a false sense of security, where the impositions of formal controls actually reduce the organization's ability to form creative solutions that are required to deal effectively with uncertainty, unpredictable conditions, and an unknown future. All the while, both frameworks continue to measure success based on the achievement of prior strategic goals and objectives thus assuming a deliberate strategic planning approach where the strategic decisions are thought to derive from that planning process.

So, while both frameworks pay closer attention to the involvement of many individuals throughout the organization, their view is better understood as an increased awareness about existing procedures to ensure they are being applied properly. It does not really recognize that many dispersed decision-makers within the organization can have a positive effect on strategic outcomes and the ongoing adaptation of business activities through autonomous (entrepreneurial) initiatives that can generate new solutions to deal with the true uncertainties that challenge our corporations, institutions, and societies. This is consistent with the broad evidence recorded in the strategy field demonstrating how many of the most important adaptive decisions are made when actions are taken deep within the organization, at times even without top management knowing about it.

There is still a 'risk' that the major ERM frameworks inadvertently may try to enforce or impose a false interpretation of the organizational decision dynamic onto a reality that operates differently from the underlying beliefs expressed in the standardized frameworks. We can put this dilemma even more simply; can the changes proposed by both COSO and ISO (which we broadly applaud), escape the gravitational pull of risk management's own history? Our argument thus far suggests that there is room for doubt, and we will explain ourselves more completely in the balance of this book.

SOMETHING TO THINK ABOUT

This chapter provides a story for understanding how risk management moved from a very narrow application to the challenges of assessing and addressing risk to a very wide-ranging and varied set of practices today. Along the way the theme of path-dependency emerged to explain how the present practices often are the consequence of conscious and unconscious decisions, happenstance, and reactions to crises. Contingency holds sway here.

We close this chapter with a short case—really, almost a parable— that provides a moment of reflection regarding the emotion, energy, and effort that have been put forward to drive the adoption of ERM programs within organizations. Perhaps surprising to some our subject is LEGO. We say *surprising* because for many years LEGO has been seen as the apotheosis of the ERM movement's ambition—a true vanguard of successfully applied modern risk management practices.

LEGO's past reflects the successful development of a strong market concept in the toy industry that led to one of the world's most recognized brands. However, an excessive belief in the possibilities of the brand and high ambitions to extend it beyond the initial core products in the toy market exceeded its resources. By 2004 the company had over-diversified into theme parks, book publishing, and various specialized toys that began to slow revenue growth and overextend the available resources, hurting the ability to generate positive cash flows. Led by Jørgen Vig Knudstorp as newly appointed CEO, the company was then revitalized sparking a rebound of proportions that might qualify as a Hans Christian Andersen fairytale, with a lesson on the value of returning the focus on sales to its core building sets. In the ensuing decade LEGO posted annual growth figures on both the top and bottom-line well in excess of 10% in a global toy market that was expected to grow below 2% per year. Along the way LEGO overtook Hasbro and Mattel to become the world's largest toy manufacturer.

As a central feature of the turnaround LEGO experimented with (and ultimately developed) a unique strategic risk management function. According to Hans Læssøe, then Head of Strategic Risk Management at LEGO, the CFO approached him in February 2006 and said: "We need some strategic risk management, don't you think?"[31] Hans Læssøe had never heard about this concept before, but as a +25-year LEGO veteran with an engineering background, he proved to be fit for purpose. Reporting back that he thought it was a fair proposition, he was ready to start. He was authorized to spend one day a week working on this idea, with a promise that LEGO would support expansions of his time commitment if and when it might be needed.

Rather than relying on more formalized descriptions of ERM, Hans Læssøe organized his work around three fundamental questions: What can hit you? How important is it? What are you going to do about it? These three questions are obviously simplified versions of the generic risk management model that underpins all the ERM frameworks. It is worth noting that the effort had a distinct strategic risk focus, knowing full well that many other functions in the organization managed the insurance contracts for productive assets and buildings, health and safety conditions, financial risk management, etc. Being housed in the Finance Department, Læssøe's engagement to develop and test out these possibilities reflected a realization that the dire economic circumstances at the time required something new to move the organization in the right direction and create a more stable economic footing.

This led to the formal establishment of a small strategic risk management function for the LEGO Group in 2007 as support for the new executive team put in place after the early struggles with declining sales and net cash inflows. While this was an evolutionary process, it eventually established a set of strategic risk management practices that seemed to work well for the Group. The Executive Committee used it as a way to be challenged on its strategic thinking and to test the robustness of proposed strategies and major investments. These efforts used a simple but effective scenario-planning framework to engage high-level executives in open discussions as well, and it eventually was adapted for application to assess all investment projects above a certain size, where groups of identified decision-makers and involved specialists would discuss potential threats and opportunities. This was supplemented with a more conventional risk management effort to identify the major enterprise risks, with a risk register of about 100 risks, to be updated, assessed, and mitigated on an ongoing basis more in line with the conventional ERM frameworks. Note that while the 'tool box' contained conventional ERM style components, it largely consisted of applying effective processes that were already in use across the various business activities of the group.[32]

With the mounting success of the revitalized organization, the need for a strategic risk management function became less obvious as time went by—the argument being, why do we need to be challenged as before, when we actually have proven to be so successful? The explosive growth became, in a sense, its own justification for trusting in the continued success of the organization. However, the forthcoming growth would have to come from internationalization beyond the traditional markets in Western Europe and North America with a substantial future growth potential lying in Asia. So, demands to make the organization more international both to attract qualified high-level executives and young smart employees became apparent to the leadership. The conclusion was to develop a more extended global governance structure with diversified headquarter locations beyond the original confines of Billund, the small Danish town where the LEGO headquarters were located.

Then in 2017, LEGO, the hitherto world-beating toy producer, had to report an unexpected drop in profits down 3% for the first half of 2017—the slowest for more than ten years.[33] As a consequence LEGO cut 1,400 jobs before the year end to scale back and create a better match between revenues and resource utilization. While Jørgen Vig Knudstorp, who had just retired as CEO to become Group Chairman, argued that the company would only do this correction as a one-time big move, he could not issue a guarantee. He further explained that the new unexpected situation was caused by the organizational growth with a more complex global management structure.[34] The company was hit by weaker demand in the established markets while the organization admittedly had grown to become too complex over the past years to support the global growth in the market.[35]

Note here that Hans Læssøe had left the company for early retirement in 2016. One might speculate that organizational complacency and challenges of dealing with success figured as factors in his decision to finally part with his long-time employer. As the slimming of the organization took place during 2017, inevitably the last remnants of people within the strategic risk management function were among those that were asked to leave the organization.

The critical observation here is that LEGO's highly lauded strategic risk management efforts were born of a crisis, but—in effect—disappeared as the result of another (minor) crisis (of managing success). Today risk management is still part of the official vocabulary in the company, but it has changed its meaning and evolved into—primarily—a compliance tool. We think this story offers (at least) three points of reflection:

1. Can risk management or ERM assure its own continuity in the face of significant organizational, governance, and external changes over time?
2. What, in fact, is the objective of risk management or ERM from the perspective of the overall progression and development of an organization?
3. If ERM is effective, should not the organization be able to better anticipate and address the essential strategic factors that affect financial results (increasing pressures from competing with cheap toys, particularly in Asian emerging markets; new inroads made by toys supported by digital technology in conventional markets; a larger complex organization structure, changes in leadership, or indeed, complacency and overconfidence).

NOTES

1 Postman, Neil (2000). *Building a Bridge to the 18th Century: How the Past Can Improve Our Future. Vintage Books*, New York.
2 For example see Fayol, H. (1949). *General and Industrial Management. Pitman Publishing*, New York.
3 A helpful review is found in Crockford, G.N. (1982). The bibliography and history of risk management: Some preliminary observations. *Geneva Papers on Risk and Insurance*, 7(23): 169–179.
4 Knight, Frank H. (1921). *Risk, Uncertainty, and Profit. Houghton Mifflin*, Boston, MA.
5 A key illustration of the early focus on measurable uncertainty can be found in Cummins, J.D. and Freifelder, L.R. (1978). Statistical analysis in Risk Management. Eight-part series appearing in *Risk Management.*
6 An influential book that had an impact on risk management thinking is Deming, W.E. (1986). *Out of the Crisis.* Center for Advanced Engineering Study, Massachusetts Institute of Technology, Cambridge, MA.
7 The first edition of David K. Eiteman and Arthur I. Stonehill's influential book on Multinational Business Finance was released in 1979.
8 Black, F. and Scholes, M. (1973). The pricing of options and corporate liabilities. *Journal of Political Economy*, 81: 637–654.
9 In 2007 the Chicago Board of Trade (CBOT) merged to form the CME Group comprised of the four exchanges, CBOT, CME, NYMEX and COMEX that offer a wide range of exchange traded derivatives contracts on global benchmark commodities and financials.
10 An early indicator of this argument for integration was Haimes, Y.Y. (1992). Toward a holistic approach to total risk management. *Geneva Papers on Risk and Insurance*, 17(64): 314–321.

11   June 2004, initial Basel II framework; Nov. 2005, Full publication of Basel II; June 2006, Comprehensive versions of full Basel II publication.

12   A fundamental early challenge for finance scholars was to explain why firms even purchased insurance or practiced risk management as theory postulated investors could manage risk through diversified investment strategies. The reconciliation of theory and practice came with Mayers, D. and Smith, Jr., C.W. (1982). On the corporate demand for insurance. *Journal of Business*, 22(2): 281–296.

13   See, for example, Nocco, B.W. and Stulz, R.M. (2006). Enterprise risk management. *Journal of Applied Corporate Finance*, 18(4): 8–20.

14   A single illustration of the many efforts to develop the ERM rationale is found in Beasley, M.S., Clune, R. and Hermanson, D.R. (2005). Enterprise risk management: An empirical analysis of factors associated with the extent of implementation. *Journal of Accounting and Public Policy*, 24(6): 521–531.

15   Some prominent examples of early and developing ERM thinking are: Beasley, M., Nunez, K. and Wright, L. (2006). Working hand in hand: Balanced scorecards and enterprise risk management. *Strategic Finance*, (March): 49–55. Dawson, M.A. (2008). Integrating compliance risk management into enterprise risk management. *Bank Accounting and Finance*, (August–September). Gordon, L.A., Loeb, M.P. and Tseng, C.Y. (2009). Enterprise risk management and firm performance: A contingency perspective. *Journal of Accounting and Public Policy*, 28(4): 301–327. Griggs, M.D. (2008). The relationship between enterprise risk management and operational risk management. *The RMA Journal*, 90(9).

16   Directive 2006/43/EC Art. 41-2b: Directive 2006/43/EC of the European Parliament and of the Council of May 17, 2006 on statutory audits of annual accounts and consolidated accounts, amending Council Directives 78/660/ EEC and 83/349/EEC and repealing Council Directive 84/253/EEC, 9.6.2006 *Official Journal of the European Union* L 157/87 https://eur-lex.europa.eu/ legal-content/EN/TXT/?uri=celex%3A32006L0043.

17   FERMA/ECIIA (2010). Guidance on the 8th EU Company Law Directive— Article 41, Guidance for boards and audit committees. www.ferma.eu/app/ uploads/2011/09/eciia-ferma-guidance-on-the-8th-eu-company-law-directive. pdf.

18   FERMA/ECIIA (2011). Guidance on the 8th EU Company Law Directive. Audit and Risk Committees News from EU Legislation and Best Practices. www.ferma.eu/app/uploads/2014/10/ECIIA_FERMA_Brochure_v8.pdf.

19   FERMA/ECIIA (2014). Guidance on the 8th EU Company Law Directive— Article 41, Guidance for boards and audit committees, Part 1. www.ferma. eu/app/uploads/2011/09/eciia-ferma-guidance-on-the-8th-eu-company-law-directive.pdf.

20   Anderson, D.J. and Eubanks, G. (2015). Leveraging COSO across the three lines of defense. *The Institute of International Auditors, COSO—Committee of Sponsoring Organizations of the Treadway Commission*. www.coso.org/ Documents/COSO-2015-3LOD.pdf.

21   Arndorfer, I. and Minto, A. (2015). The 'four' lines of defence model for financial institutions. *Financial Stability Institute, Occasional Paper No. 11, Bank for International Settlements*. www.bis.org/fsi/fsipapers11.pdf.

22   Basel Committee on Banking Supervision, Guidelines: Corporate Governance Principles for Banks, Bank for International Settlements, July 2015.

23   Power, M. (2004). The risk management of everything. *The Journal of Risk Finance*, 5(3): 58–65.

24   Power, M. (2009). The risk management of nothing. *Accounting, Organization and Society*, 34(6–7): 849–855.

25 Beltratti, A. and Stulz, R.M. (2009). *Why Did Some Banks Perform Better During the Credit Crisis? A Cross-Country Study of the Impact of Governance and Regulation* (No. w15180). *National Bureau of Economic Research*.

26 Bromiley, P., McShane, M., Nair, A. and Rustambekov, E. (2015). Enterprise risk management: Review, critique, and research. *Long Range Planning*, 48(4): 265–276.

27 A good article that makes our point is Gold, J. (2006). Reducing a company's beta: A novel way to increase shareholder value. *Journal of Applied Corporate Finance*, 18(4): 110–113.

28 RiskMinds (2009). Risk Managers' Survey. www.moorecarter.co.uk/RiskMinds%20 2009%20Risk%20Managers'%20Survey%20Report.19March2010.pdf.

29 Enterprise Risk Management: Integrating Strategy and Performance. 2017, COSO and ISO 31000:2018, ISO.

30 Henriksen, Per (2018). *Enterprise Risk Management: Rationaler og Paradokser i en Moderne Ledelsesteknologi*. PhD Dissertation, Doctoral School of Business and Management, Copenhagen Business School.

31 Hans Læssøe: The LEGO Group implementation of SRM, in Andersen, T.J. (ed.) (2015). *The Routledge Companion to Strategic Risk Management*.

32 Mark L. Frigo and Hans Læssøe (2012). Strategic risk management at the LEGO Group. *Strategic Finance*.

33 Quartz: https://qz.com/1069520/lego-announces-layoffs-after-reporting-an-unexpected-drop-in-sales-and-profit/.

34 CNBC: www.cnbc.com/2017/09/05/toymaker-lego-to-cut-8-percent-of-staff-as-sales-decline.html.

35 *The Guardian*: www.theguardian.com/business/2017/sep/05/lego-to-axe-1400-jobs.

3 Standards and practices

To wish was to hope, and to hope was to expect.

Jane Austen[1]

We believe the sudden appearance of Jane Austen may prove disquieting—if not alarming—to our more conventionally minded risk management colleagues, and we further observe that while this quotation has more than one interpretation, it also shines a light on our views regarding human behavior under conditions of uncertainty.[2]

This chapter focuses on present day risk management approaches, and our intention here is to put the actual practices alongside the current ERM standards. Do the practices align with the processes portrayed in the ERM frameworks, and if not, does a misalignment tell us something? We believe it is fair to assume that we would not develop an entire chapter around a compare-and-contrast look at standards and practices if the answer to the preceding question was 'no.' Indeed, it is our contention that the misalignment tells us a fair bit.

In this light, the Austen quote offers an underlying percussive beat in this chapter. The efforts to standardize risk management are, we could say, a *wish* that becomes a *hope* once the standard exists and becomes a living thing, or when it prompts an effort to comply with external expectations.[3] That *hope* becomes an *expectation*, which is to say that supporters of the standards expect or assume that an intended positive outcome—the wish—is the end result. Here, Austen's 'expectation' is our focus—is what we expect ERM to look like exactly what we see in living, breathing organizations that adopt the frameworks?

Austen's insight also echoes in observations made throughout the remainder of this book. Later we will see that humans are inclined to rely on mental heuristics, or simple rules of thumb based on past experiences and interpretations. Among the more powerful consequences of this is our inclination to only see what we want to see (often referred to as *confirmation bias*), so we frequently come to expect particular outcomes—not because they arise from rigorous scientific investigation or critical thinking, but rather because it is what we wish to see happen. Chapters 4 and 5 will be influenced by the insights derived from this 'wishing, hoping, and expecting.'

But, now on to the present state of affairs.

RISK LEADERS, RISK LEADERSHIP

As a first order of business, we want to explain the distinction between the terms *risk leadership* and *risk management*.[4] Risk management has been discussed previously, but risk leaders and risk leadership have only made a cameo appearance thus far.

Risk leadership refers to situations where a certain understanding of risk and uncertainty—along with other skills, knowledge, and abilities—is put in the service of persuading, inspiring, envisioning, communicating, championing, and initiating; where, as a point of contrast, risk management relates to the more technical aspects of planning, coordinating, executing, budgeting, and monitoring. The distinction is not sharp in practice as risk leaders also tend to have risk management and leadership elements to their jobs and vice versa; or to put it even more generally, managing and leading are part of nearly everyone's job. Still, it is important to maintain a bit of separation—at least for discussion purposes—because there is an emerging type of risk manager whose primary responsibilities can be better described as leading on assessing and addressing risk rather than managing risk. Further, understanding the leader/leadership phenomenon opens a window into a wider (and differently ordered) view of what is going on in the world of risk management today.

Slightly confusingly, risk leadership presently has at least three usages: 1) the important notion that top individuals in organizations, who may have many non-risk-oriented responsibilities, often have expectations placed upon them to provide direction and *tone at the top* in order to create an environment that can support the implementation of an effective risk management program; 2) multiparty situations where entities and organizations must find ways to coordinate efforts in response to common risk exposures; and 3) wide-ranging situations where any manager or individual moves beyond basic managerial tasks to lead in addressing risks that have an impact on their job, but which also may extend beyond that person's specific area of responsibility.

For our purposes, consider the following building-block look at risk management and risk leadership, risk managers, and risk leaders. Start with the notion that within everyone's job there are activities and responsibilities that can be seen as risk management (dealing with risks associated with planning, staffing, and allocating resources for a new initiative), but everyone will encounter situations where the term *risk leadership* is a better descriptor of that person's response or responsibility (taking initiative to coordinate across business units when an issue of common concern arises).

Add to this, then, that within the employee ranks will commonly be found individuals with specialized knowledge for dealing with particular categories of risk, e.g., financial risks, security risks, health and safety risks, etc. Those individuals are referred to as *Risk Managers* (sometimes 'technical' risk managers, as we have noted) and indeed they will have a risk leadership role to play as well. Then, in a most general sense, top managers and boards will have risk leadership responsibilities, and let us note that from a conceptual standpoint these individuals are **the** *risk leader(s)* of the organization.

However, in a growing number of organizations practicalities dictate that some additional individual (or group of individuals) be present within the top levels—a person (or persons) with a deeper understanding of technical risk management and a higher level of general strategic management and leadership capability—a person or group designated with organization-wide responsibilities for risk. These new risk managers have many titles (Chief Risk Officer, CRO, is commonly employed), but here we choose to label these individuals *Risk Leaders* (capitalized as a way to differentiate them from the general notion that, say, the CEO is a risk leader). To be clear, the presence of a singular and identifiable Risk Leader is neither a necessary nor sufficient condition for the newer approaches to risk management. However, it does seem to be the case that most organizations who embrace a more comprehensive approach find that top management must add an individual, or a dedicated group to lead on the risk management efforts.

For purposes of clarity the Risk Leader (or group) will be defined here as 'that individual or group occupying the highest rank within an organization and having express responsibilities for leading on and managing risks.' And as noted, while reality does lead to overlaps, individuals with somewhat narrower and more technical responsibilities will be referred to here as risk managers (capitalized as *Risk Managers* where relevant or where distinctions need to be made). The proposed typology can be expressed as in the following box.

> *All managers and employees = risk management and risk leadership responsibilities*
> *Specialists in risk management = risk managers who also have leadership responsibilities*
> *Expressly designated risk leader(s) = risk leaders who also have risk management duties*
> *The executive team and board = risk leaders with risk leadership responsibilities*

Further explaining the emergence of the risk leader in organizations has revealed that there is a clear emphasis on the engagement of top management in setting policy and a guiding tone. All the while the general expectation remains that all managers and employees are managers of the risks that arise within the scope of their duties as well as an expectation that there are various technical Risk Managers located throughout the organization. Yet, there was/is still a weak spot in the general structure of such an approach. Put simply, in most organizations top managers tend not to have quite enough technical understanding of modern risk management (neither do they have the time to oversee detailed risk practices). Conversely, while lower level managers (even technical Risk Managers) may have specific depth of expertise in particular areas, they are not adequately positioned to understand organization-wide risk management goals and practices, to integrate wide-ranging technical efforts, and to exploit potential synergistic possibilities.

As a consequence, most organizations have found it necessary to install—indeed, have been required to in many regulated industries—at a minimum, a risk information/communication traffic warden or a traffic team. Their role is to organize, manage, and monitor risk reporting and assessment systems so proper information—in proper forms and with proper timing—is flowing upward to the top management team, and down/outward to the organization.

Furthermore, these individuals or groups must assure that various risk management measures are effectively implemented in conformance with the organizational risk policy and possible legal requirements. As noted previously, we label this individual (or group) the Risk Leader, though it should be made clear that this term also connotes a function as much as a specific individual(s).

As is set out in the previous chapter, the field of risk management has passed through a period of rapid transformation since the start of the century interrupted by extreme events such as the 2008 financial crisis. Change has not been seamless, neither has it been comprehensive, and advancement is far from uniform. Some small organizations have highly complex risk management systems in place, while larger organizations may have no formalized practices whatsoever, and vice versa. Some organizations have a Risk Leader, but no Risk Managers, and some organizations display the exact opposite.

In spite (or because) of this situation, we believe there is something beyond pure circumstance in these widely different approaches to risk management, including decisions not to formally introduce risk management at all, or to pursue risk management in unique ways. Shortly, we will argue here that different approaches to risk management are not just due to mere circumstance, lack of organizational sophistication, or technical knowledge, but are influenced by institutionalized beliefs, professional institutions, policy-makers and regulators as well as unique individual factors. In other words, we think there is something of an organizing idea behind the differences.

One of the more interesting and relevant issues is the question of what risk leaders are supposed to know and do. Since the Risk Leader is a new phenomenon, there is not a clearly delineated job description and there is not an obvious pathway of preparation for such positions. One thing does seem clear from the evidence, however. Becoming a Risk Leader is not just a matter of scaling up a traditional risk manager's work. This is not meant as a disrespectful comment on the highly talented Risk Managers in the field. It is simply to say that historic risk management functions have been judged on operational and technical performance and rather less emphatically evaluated on the basis of general management and strategic leadership skills. Furthermore, despite a common DNA, the various technical specialists do not necessarily possess a solid understanding of other technical risk specializations. The result of this is that, with only some notable exceptions, the existing pool of Risk Managers has not been teeming with candidates for officer or director level (Risk Leader) positions.

But to be fair to Risk Managers, consider this issue from the opposite direction. A Risk Leader might be selected from a cadre of top managers or top experts in other areas (finance, operations, IT), and in some situations this may make sense. For example, an assistant CFO of a bank might be well-acquainted with the core business risks in this particular industry and thus might serve with distinction as a Risk Leader. Nevertheless, it is arguable that the pool of candidates, broadly conceived, would be strong in general and strategic management and leadership skills but weaker on an understanding of the detailed risk management concepts and principles, as well as the various technical specializations therein.

Early insights

The growth of modern risk management/leadership has not been free of political influences since much is at stake for professional communities, organizations, consultants, academics, and various technical experts. Thus, over recent years we have witnessed a kind of capture-the-flag competition, whereby ERM is variously defined through the lens of audit, finance, insurance, legal, operations, and security, among other perspectives. This is understandable, and to be fair, the risk management idea does include all of these important views.

Nevertheless, there is a bigger, more inclusive, defining idea that exists today. We might characterize that bigger idea as one where:

- Risk Management is explicitly connected to the organization's strategic goals and informed in accordance with governance and compliance expectations.
- Top management and boards have an express role in establishing an organizational policy toward risk and assuring that performance expectations are met.
- With the assistance of technical risk experts within the organization, all decision-makers are risk managers within the scope of their responsibilities.
- While philosophically one might say that both the CEO and the chairman of the board share the title of 'Risk Leader' practicalities dictate that one individual (or group) of sufficiently elevated status has overall responsibility for leading, coordinating, educating, communicating, and managing the organization-wide risk management efforts.

These four bullet points seem quite similar to the generic ERM framework, but a closer reading indicates (we hope) some breathing spaces where a different way of thinking about risk management can emerge. More on this later.

For the moment, it is that '(an) individual(s) of sufficiently elevated status' who is/are the present subject(s) of interest here. Who is this person or people? From where and what backgrounds do they come? What knowledge, skills, and abilities are necessary to perform this role?

There are two central reasons why these questions are important. First, there do not appear to be simple answers—indeed, there is very little literature on the subject—so searching for answers would seem to shine a light on the entire configuration of modern risk management. Second, in certain sectors regulations and other requirements have allowed the demand for these individuals to outstrip our ability to understand the specific requirements the role would seem to demand, and the types of individuals needed to succeed in these positions.

We took it upon ourselves to conduct a small exploratory survey to help shape a better understanding of the Risk Leader, the role of that executive function, the background and preparation for that role, and the current and future developmental needs of that individual.[5] In addition to asking about perspectives on the individual Risk Leader, the questions were also geared to investigate the Risk Leader as a function. In the following we look at what we consider to be key insights from our inquiries.

The problem in defining and finding 'Risk Leaders'

There are some inherent problems with the title Risk Leader, though it is a term that is increasing in visibility. For evaluative purposes: "A Risk Leader is the highest-ranking individual within an organization that has express responsibilities for assessing and addressing the widest range of risks."

Even this definition has limitations. What does it mean to be high ranking, and what does it mean to have responsibilities for the widest range of risks? Given these problems, the pre-survey phase expanded our description and then an organization-by-organization search process was undertaken to find the person within the most prominent organizations in Minnesota that would most closely fit with the proposed description. So we included additional consideration of:

- Whether the person(s) in question were centrally situated within the organization (and with the exception of a few explainable circumstances, were not in a specific functional area).
- Whether the person(s) were of senior level ranking (with titles like director, senior vice president, etc.).
- Whether the person(s) had a direct report to one or more of the following high-level audiences: CEO, Executive committee, board, or board sub-committee.
- Whether the person(s) were not exclusively associated with a single technical specialization (insurance buying, derivative markets, or lean operations, for example).

Our investigation ultimately identified 93 organizations and individuals that seemed to have positions commensurate with the outlined description criteria and they all received a designed questionnaire. Over 60% of these senior executives completed and returned the surveys with usable responses. The surveying experience underscored the challenges of identifying the Risk Leader (or Risk Leader function). Some respondents were found, through their responses, not to be performing the role defined here after all and thus had to be discarded from the subsequent analysis. Just to give a flavor of the complexity involved in determining the proper individual risk leaders, consider some of the titles held by the persons that were found to actually fit our Risk Leader description:

- Chief Finance Officer
- Chief Risk Officer (the predominant title, primarily found in regulated organizations)
- Director of Enterprise Risk Management
- Senior Manager Enterprise Risk Management
- Director of Insurance and Risk Management
- Director of Information Security
- Director of Environment, Safety and Risk Management
- Director of Internal Audit
- Director of Risk Management
- Director of Business Risk and Process Improvement
- Manager, Enterprise Risk & Insurance
- Firm Director
- Partner, National Capability leader for Risk Assurance ERM Services
- Risk Management Officer
- Safety/Risk Management
- Treasury Director-Risk Management
- Vice President Risk Services
- Vice President, Business Risk Management
- Vice President, Risk Management & Legal Operations.

To whom do Risk Leaders report?

There was a wide degree of variation from our expected reporting relationship ('reports to CEO, board, or board committee'). Respondents most frequently reported to the CFO, closely followed by reporting to the CEO, the Audit Committee, the General Counsel, the Board of Directors, but the CAO, CIO, and COO were also mentioned. Some responders described a dual role where they had responsibilities directly to the Board, while also occupying a position as a member of the Executive Team. While far from a unique positioning, this suggests a responsibility representing two reasonably distinct perspectives on risk.

Motivations for ERM adoption

One of the central questions in the risk management field today relates to an organization's motivation to adopt ERM, and the survey results were consistent with preexisting studies. These inquiries have shown that regulatory or industry requirements play a very large role in the adoption of ERM, especially in already highly regulated sectors like banking. Less frequently, adoption comes down to strategic business considerations or to the influence of an internal *champion*. Finally, catastrophic events, or near-death experiences have been shown to drive organizations toward the introduction and development of ERM.

There is an interesting reason why this matter is important. As ISO 31000 argues, ERM is less likely to be successful if it is not consistent with an organization's culture and values. One way to interpret this is that ERM is unlikely to achieve its intended purpose if an organization adopts ERM only because it is required to, or if ERM is applied only in bad times to rein clear of the immediate dangers. Another implication of the ISO view is that ERM invariably will have to look quite different from organization to organization since it must be implemented in line with the firm-specific cultural fabric.

There is a third issue, which is widely commented on but not well researched. Regardless of motivation, how specifically does ERM begin to be implemented within an organization? Some practitioner literature seems to show that an individual of influence within the organization needs to take a significant leadership role for this to happen. This, it is argued, is partly due to the challenge of introducing a new and organization-wide change. It is also due to the difficulties in getting managers and people in general to subscribe to these wide-ranging changes if there is no visible and active support from members of top management and/or the board.

We asked respondents if they knew who took the initiatin or leadership responsibility for promoting ERM within their organizations. The interesting finding was that the Risk Leader, him/herself, self-reported as filling this role in nearly 20% of the cases. The CEO, CFO, Board Chairman, and a few other director level individuals were also identified as instrumental drivers of ERM.

We summarize here by offering a question that will get some attention later on. Let us phrase it this way. If, in fact, it is true that ERM and Risk

Leaders enter the picture because: 1) regulators require their presence, or 2) a catastrophe suddenly incentivizes the organization, or 3) an internal champion promotes and leads on advancing ERM and the Risk Leader function, then there is likely a key question about the organization's 'ERM origination story.' Other studies and observed experiences strongly support the idea that the commitment of top-level executive(s) to ERM and the Risk Leaders is a necessary condition for successful ERM implementation. If true, both motives 1) and 2) are problematic, and in the case of motive 3), a large number of respondents indicate that they had to be their own champions, which suggests that there was no prior champion or top management support and therefore the primary motive most likely was either 1) or 2).

By what means do Risk Leaders add value?

This is a key question with both philosophical and practical implications. Philosophically, what is that unique combination of knowledge/skill/ability that differentiates a Risk Leader from other organizational leaders? If there is no difference between them, the question might well be asked: Why are organizations—or why should they be—hiring such people? More practically, from both a professional development and an academic standpoint, the question could be framed differently: How does one prepare to become an effective Risk Leader and what then are the proper measures or indicators that identify risk leadership effectiveness?

The responses to what the distinguishing characteristics of a risk leader are were wide-ranging, but they might be organized according to the following categories: Technical Knowledge, General Managerial Acumen, Personal Skills and Attributes, and Intangible Qualities, as shown in the following box.

Skills, knowledge, ability	# of responses
Technical knowledge	30
Risk knowledge, Risk management knowledge, statistics, audit, project management, teaching.	
General management acumen	88
Business knowledge, strategic thinking, industry knowledge, organization knowledge, knowledge of relevant laws/regulations, change management, delegating skills, communication.	

Personal skills and attributes   44

Facilitation, leadership, listening skills, critical thinking, collaboration, experiences, influencing, consensus building, people skills, sales skills.

Intangible qualities   45

Adaptability, see the big picture, curiosity, deal with ambiguity, credibility, creativity, trustworthy, resilience, attention to detail, calm under pressure, challenge the status quo, confidence, diligence, emotional intelligence, ethics.

The indicated numbers of respondents to each category are merely the sum of those that cited those possibilities under the specific heading. However, it is intriguing that the least commonly cited category was Technical Knowledge (and within that category risk knowledge and risk management knowledge were cited by fewer than 30% of those respondents). This is curious as the differentiator between Risk Leaders and other leaders would seem related to their technical competency in risk and affiliated subjects. If that is not the case, what is then a Risk Leader's distinctive capability?

Reflecting on this, we think there are some obvious caveats to the preceding observations. Perhaps the respondents are actually saying that they rely on technical experts to answer those questions, so it is not that they are unconversant in the technical aspects of risk management, but rather that they do not perceive themselves as one of the technical experts. Furthermore, there may simply not have been enough information available to define risk leadership knowledge, skills, and abilities for the respondents to be able to formulate appropriate answers. Notwithstanding these limitations, we find the responses to be interesting.

THE WIDER ERM SCENE

The preceding sections provide some insights into the Risk Leader as a newcomer to the risk management world—clearly there is a lot yet to learn. But what is the wider story about current risk management practices? The instinctive answer would be to say that ISO and COSO are effectively stating what modern risk management should look like, which is not a surprising response. However, what do we know about the actual practices?

One obvious source of evidence is the ever-growing number of studies and surveys that are now produced each year in the risk management world. A cynical observer might say that the producers of such surveys are not really reacting to a growing underlying interest but are promoting the growth of risk management adherents. True enough, but this is something to always keep in mind when considering surveying results. Having noted that, just to provide a glimpse of the range of sources for survey-based insights, a selection of the surveys we reviewed included:

- North Carolina State University: Survey of Risk Assessment Practices
- Deloitte: Global Risk Management Survey—10th edition
- RIMS: 2017 Enterprise Risk Management Survey
- McKinsey & Company: Enterprise Risk Management Practices
- Aon: Global Risk Management Survey
- The Open Group: Risk Management Practices Survey
- AICPA: The State of Risk Oversight: An Overview of Enterprise Risk Management.
- Protiviti: Enterprise Risk Management
- Ingenta Connect: How do you deal with operational risk? A survey
- UONBI: A survey of internal auditors risk management practices in banking
- FEI Canada: 2018 Risk Management Practices Survey
- HSBC: Risk Management Survey
- Citibank: FX risk management practices
- KPMG: Risk Management Survey/Operational Risk Management
- NAFSA: Risk Management Survey Results
- Wells Fargo: Risk Management Practices Survey.

Looking across a wide range of surveys it seems possible to discern a distinct—and due to their varying orientations—arguably indicative depiction of actual current practices.

Aspirations

One finding that seems consistent across almost all the studies is that organizations aspire to comply with either ISO or COSO (and sometimes, though rarely, both), which suggests rather strongly that there is a conscious view within the leading organizations that compliance with these guidelines is a desired outcome. Yet, the organizations rarely identify themselves as fully compliant (or, to use a common phrase, have failed to reach risk management maturity), and several possible explanations come to mind as to why this might be the case:

1. It is just too early. ERM is still new enough that organizations simply have not had adequate time to achieve full compliance. As an aggregate or composite explanation for organizations this is a plausible view.
2. There is some natural or logical sequencing to the adoption of ERM practices, so the intentions might be strong, but the implementation is simply a lengthy process, irrespective of the potential effectiveness of the concept.
3. There may be some inherent issues with the COSO/ISO guidelines that are problematic when they are transposed into complex organizations operating in turbulent environments. We think there might be something to this, but there is a need to investigate further.
4. Completing large organization-wide changes is inherently problematic and linked to fundamental 'change-management' issues. So, the challenges may not be specific to ERM but are general artefacts of implementing large-scale projects—an insight that ISO seems to have recognized in its recent update.

It is worthwhile to briefly ponder these alternative explanations. It certainly is a possibility that all four explanations may be contributing factors. Indeed, we are inclined to believe that. So, one conclusion might be that we just need to be patient. Things will eventually work themselves out. A slightly different response might be, however, that while it is all good and well that organizations will eventually achieve ERM maturity, we might still wonder if it was worth it; if it was a good thing to do.

Additionally, embedded in all four answers is an implied sense that organization-wide change initiatives are, by definition, extremely difficult undertakings that require a great deal of time. Given some of our previously stated concerns about *time*, we might wonder if full maturity is practically achievable. Mind you, traveling along the journey toward maturity—but never quite arriving at the destination—might be nevertheless worthwhile.

So, the journey itself may be the actual benefit of ERM, but we return to a point raised previously in this book. There is not much empirical evidence that ERM adds value to organizations. This is a disturbing finding, and—in fact—it seems to contradict theoretical arguments for ERM. To us, there are two possible conclusions:

1. Supporting evidence will be found eventually, or
2. The theories are wrong or are—for all intents and purposes— unachievable in the real world of organizations.

There is a third possibility, which is a variation on #2. The theory is internally consistent, but it has mis-specified what risk management is. We raise this particular possibility because we actually think this could be the right interpretation. Obviously this point receives quite a bit of attention in Chapters 4 and 5, but let us mention just a couple of things here.

It seems likely to us that the risk management measures necessary to add value to organizations do not derive particularly from systems and processes (though controls have a role in a well-managed company). Rather, we suspect that measures that enhance responsiveness, flexibility, critical thinking, and innovation are likely to be the effects that add value. These objectives do not receive featured attention in most ERM modeling. We wonder, then, whether a) risk management is mis-specified, i.e. the model is wrong or has shortcomings, leading to b) the wrong things being measured and monitored.

Although different interpretations of this issue may be forcibly argued, our sense is that while a number of factors might explain why it takes so long to implement a fully compliant ERM program, our view is that we suspect it could be impossible to actually reach full ERM maturity, and doing so might not be worth the effort. We do not actually have empirical evidence that ERM adds value to organizations and thus we may be engaged in a faith-based exercise when we embark on an ERM implementation.

Actual practices

Before providing a summarizing view to research findings, we need to talk about organizations that do not get captured in most risk management surveying. Obviously there could be large organizations that simply ignore survey questionnaires, but only at the margins is this an issue. Rather, we are thinking about small- to medium-sized organizations who either do not respond or are not in surveying target groups. This actually represents far-and-away the largest segment of organizations in the world. Are we to assume that they do not practice risk management?

Well, they may not be officially subscribing to ERM methodologies, but we do not believe that nothing is happening. Indeed, the ancient maps with *terra incognita* featured prominently seems an apt analogy here. For one thing, it is certain that many such organizations have at least part-time technical risk managers (insurance-buying, safety and security). Further, many organizations have risk management imposed upon them (workplace safety regulations, insurance requirements, auditing/tax requirements), so someone is likely practicing risk management, even if they are not quite aware that is what they are doing. We are pretty confident that a case can be made that a lot of risk management is being practiced in small- to medium-sized organizations.

A completely unanswerable question at present, however, is whether small- to medium-sized organizations are doing a good job of managing risks. A real debate would be necessary to determine what 'doing a good job' even means. And then someone would have to undertake an arduous effort to gather information from organizations that historically do not answer surveys. One thing we would want to clarify, however, is that smaller organizations do not have great capacity to withstand large shocks in the way that a large firm can. But, this lack of risk-bearing capacity is not a risk management failure, nor even due to a failure to practice risk management. It is simply a matter of size and scale. It is highly probable that top managers in small- to medium-sized firms actually think a lot about uncertainty and likely take steps to improve their resilience. They just do not have the resources to do much about their exposure to big impact events. And, there is at least a chance that the CEO of a medium-sized manufacturer has a more holistic sensibility about organizational risks than do CEOs of large multinational organizations.

Let us turn to the firms that do answer surveys. Results from these surveys show reasonably consistently that larger organizations are far more likely to exhibit evidence of advancing maturity with respect to ISO/COSO than smaller ones, but this may only reveal that compliance requires significant resources, or that small-large organizations have less of a need for formal processes. It is also clear that something approaching compliance is seen far more among private sector firms than in the public sector, nonprofit sectors, multilateral organizations, charitable institutions, and professional associations. There is a size/scale dimension to the reasons behind lower levels of adoption, but other factors seem to matter as well.

To the degree that an ERM—let us call it—*approach* is found outside of the largest firms, the explanation tends to align with the motives identified previously: 1) a disaster has prompted the organizational interest in risk management, 2) the organization operates in a highly regulated industry that requires certain risk management practices, and/or 3) an internal champion has argued for or introduced a more comprehensive approach to risk management. Absent any one of the three motives, we believe organizations are unlikely to adopt ERM.

Consistent with the previous chapter's story, many or most organizations across all sectors practice some forms of technical risk management. Insurance buying is a common focus, but other forms of financial risk management, safety and security, legal liability risk management are widely observed as well. Our overview and analysis of risk management history, however, does not identify with precision how the process occurs whereby organizations begin to integrate the technical risk management functions; how even basic technical risk management is specifically introduced. We are going to take a leap here and say that at this micro-level, it probably remains the case that mandates, disasters, or championing probably hold as the key motives even there.

In organizations that have adopted an ERM approach, the following features are fairly widely reported:

1. Success in moving toward full implementation of ERM is highly dependent on the buy-in and active support of top management and the board.

2. There are linkages between the technical risk management functions but no strong evidence of other forms of linkages across functional silos. That is to say, if a manager has the word 'risk' on his/her business card, there is a reasonable likelihood of communication and cooperation with other people that hold similar business cards, whereas other linkages are not as apparent or visible.

3. In larger organizations, particular associations are sometimes observed across the areas of compliance, CSR, risk, sustainability, and strategic planning. Corporate governance tends to be an issue of common concern in all these areas.

4. Larger ERM-oriented organizations often express the view that all employees have a role in managing risks, but do not report in any detail how this is being implemented, incentivized, and monitored in practice, if at all.

5. Point 4 suggests that there must be some methods for systematic requirements for risk reporting and risk communication, but those methods, if they exist, are not clearly revealed or displayed in detailed studies and surveys.

6. The ERM frameworks and the adopted ERM approaches to risk reporting are often widely divergent. A standard template suggests a Risk Office into which the technical risk managers report, and out of which communication flows to provide guidance for the organization as a whole, and into which flows information that in turn informs top management and the board. Very few organizations match that idealized template.

7. The ISO/COSO framing provides encouragement for ERM to be in full alignment with an organization's culture and values, and there is evidence that alignment between espoused and actual values is

important. However, this issue remains largely unexplored terrain, because the meaning of 'alignment with values' and a description of how that actually works are rarely considered in surveys and other studies.

8. There is emphasis in the ERM guidelines to determine risk appetite and tolerance as critical to implement proper risk adjusted decisions in the organization. The reported interpretations and implementations of these concepts, however, are rather unclear, and there are probably many more practical questions than answers to their proposed utility and value.

9. There is evidence that many firms try to adopt a risk management perspective in innovation processes, environmental assessment, planning and strategy formulation, but practices are not consistent (or evenly applied) across organizations.

10. There are expressions of acute interest around global risks and the exposures derived from operating in diverse foreign environments, but there is not much evidence on what is actually being 'done' beyond specific activities, such as complying with the Foreign Corrupt Practices Act and purchasing specialized insurance covers for country-specific risk.

What emerges from the survey findings is a picture that confirms a growing interest in ERM and an increasing number of organizations that aspire to comply with the ERM guidelines. It seems to confirm the central idea that the ERM approach is becoming part of the business vocabulary through professional promotion and intensified policy initiatives.

Alongside this summary status, we must remind ourselves that these insights only can be applied in a meaningful way to large corporations in developed countries, that only a few organizations have closed in on the ERM approach in its fullest manifestation. Even among the most ambitious of these organizations, the adopted practices are quite different after allowing for common elements that form the skeletal structure. It is worth reflecting on why this is so and map—if that is the right word—these inconsistencies with an aim to understand their existence.

Finally—and this has already gotten some attention—we observe that some of the most advanced ERM adopters have discontinued their efforts despite evidence of success and acclaim (LEGO, for example). Shifts in leadership, commercial challenges, organizational transformations, mergers and acquisitions, etc.—all these factors can play a role and may explain the changing emphasis on ERM. Nevertheless, this phenomenon is noted with sufficient frequency that it may call into question the sustainability of the ERM approaches.

An evaluation of risk management practices has shown something of a separation between principles and practices. However, we believe that narratives can trump a listing of general observations, so a couple of illustrations of the key points that have emerged so far may be helpful. Some of these examples have been observed 'up close' by the authors themselves, but they are still broadly representative of the way risk management is adopted in general. Furthermore, most of the illustrations present fairly well-known, globally oriented organizations where readers can verify things independently. First, however, a few comments to frame the narratives that follow.

The first decade of this millennium saw many attempts to advance enterprise-wide risk management approaches arguing that ERM is imperative for success in a dynamic environment. Yet, we should reflect on the true motivation behind these promotional efforts. Do they reflect heart-felt attempts to avoid the adverse effects of economic havoc, gaining quick recognition by adhering to an established risk standard, or are they true conscious exercises to facilitate maneuvering in unknown terrain? These reflect quite different, though understandable intentions.

Whatever the key motivational impetus is, the adoption of the ERM framework initially sounded reasonably easy, logical, and straightforward with everything set up around formal processes and a structured risk reporting system.[6] The main thrust was to create an integrated overview of all major risks and eliminate assumed inefficiencies associated with diverse risk functions in isolated silos. A common risk language with explicit risk appetite statements would guide proactive investments to secure proper risk-adjusted returns while achieving the planned strategic objectives. All of this was refined as a philosophy of a careful forward-looking examination of risks that might affect business performance and taking remedies to avoid major disruptive incidents.

The intentions make a lot of sense because it is smart to think about the future and how we might be able to deal with it, but it also has limitations since it only deals with things that can be identified in advance, i.e., it is not geared to deal with unexpected developments. Under uncertain and unpredictable conditions, any of the contingency plans will fall short. So, even if the risk management process is transparent, broadly communicated, and involving the whole organization, it may be unable to respond to extreme unexpected events such as, say, a financial crisis.

Much was learned, the hard way, in the aftermath of the 2008 financial crisis particularly about the potential effects of judgmental biases, but the risk management discourse gradually reversed itself toward old concerns that insufficient information was afforded to support risk governance, thus requiring greater efforts at extending internal reporting and control processes. This was a convenient reversion to the mainstream ERM perspective where the risk management community could promote the claimed benefits of ERM-based risk controls.[7] The underlying assumptions seemed substantially unchanged and generally unfazed by the experiences from the 2008 financial crisis. (Remember, though, that both COSO and ISO did issue subsequent updates.)

The eventually accepted story was about creating shareholder value by mitigating risks, consolidating risk reporting, and eliminating inefficient risk management silos. This suggested that any implementation shortfalls were rooted in insufficient standard reporting practices and failure to formulate proper risk appetite statements as some of the core beliefs held by professional associations engaged in the 'selling' of ERM as indispensable. As a point of contrast to the official story, we offer two very different examples that provide: 1) a different take on what happens in organizations with strong commitments to ERM when 'things change,' and 2) some insights into what we will consider key features of our view of risk management.

CARLSBERG

Carlsberg—the international brewer—has enjoyed a reputation for excellence in risk management. As is typical for a public company, the Carlsberg Group Supervisory Board holds the ultimate responsibility for internal controls and risk management through the Executive Committee (ExCom), which delegates execution to the Audit Committee.[8] As then Head of Internal Audit, Vibeke Aggerholm used her professional experience to develop a unique, proactive, and strategic risk management approach for the ExCom over the period 2010–2014. She was a Registered Public Accountant, had worked with EY and other major corporations, and was a board member of the Institute of Internal Auditors (IIA). Her professional background supported the implementation of a group-wide risk management framework to systematically identify, analyze, and evaluate major corporate exposures. The company also had an official risk management function mainly focused on traditional insurance-buying to cover the effects of potential accidents and operational breakdowns.[9]

The annual risk management process engaged local business units in workshops to identify major risks and remedy potential performance effects using techniques like risk heat maps and risk mitigation plans to support the achievement of short- and long-term strategic objectives. This process also brought local market opportunities to the attention of the ExCom. The total risk management process identified major financial, compliance, operational, and strategic risks with financial exposures handled by the finance functions, compliance risks by accounting and legal, and operational risks by the operating entities all reporting their risks to internal audit.

High risks identified in the heat map would require mitigation plans with strict deadlines managed by vice presidents with business responsibilities and the action plans were monitored quarterly. Emergent risks were identified in the business units and reported to internal audit. Hence, the risk management process entailed different functions, engaged local entities, and ascribed to many features of the ERM frameworks adopting conventional analytical and reporting tools.

The 2015 Annual Report lists a number of high-risk issues identified for the coming year as well as for the ensuing three-year period including immediate effects of a weakening Russian economy, increased regulation, and changes in pricing and trading terms. The longer-term strategic risks considered were the poor public image of beer, increasing taxation, and regulatory restrictions.[10]

In February 2015, on the same day as the Carlsberg Group reported declining sales and earnings for the second year in a row, it announced that CEO Jørgen Buhl Rasmussen, would retire and be replaced by Cees't Hart, then CEO of Royal Friesland Campina, the first non-Dane to take the helm at Carlsberg. Rasmussen had been credited with the successful turnaround of Carlsberg in the European markets and growth in Asia, but the weak demand in Russia proved too compelling and concerning for top management.[11]

A central question here might be why the risk management process had been unable to find effective responses to deal with these widely recognized strategic risk factors. Was it because the product of risk identification processes was a rationalization of effects already in motion showing that emergent risks are hard to observe in advance and generate timely responses to? Was it because a three-year time horizon reduces the motivation to respond until it is too late? Or, does it reflect a general shortcoming of the ERM system in identifying and dealing with events that are hard to see in advance due to an unpredictable business environment? Or even, might one wonder whether ERM did present the evidence but it was discarded or ignored? We obviously do not have the answers, but the questions remain highly relevant.

After the change of top management, Vibeke Aggerholm assumed the position of CFO for Carlsberg Italy, and the unique strategic risk management approach she had developed was folded into the conventional (technical) risk management function.[12] Those combined risk management practices appear to have continued, though clearly the positioning of ERM changed. As a side note, it is interesting that under this new configuration, an employee in the Carlsberg Breweries A/S was awarded 'Risk Manager of the Year' by DARIM (the Danish Risk Management Association) in December 2015.

We might speculate about the effects of the change in leadership where the strategic risk management process—developed and led by a Risk Leader—was integrated with the traditional risk management process. One could imagine some challenges associated with such an organizational transition. As an interesting corollary it is noted that the company subsequently recruited for new risk leadership roles including positions of Global Group Information Security Manager (April 2018) and Head of Crisis Management (October 2018) indicating an apparent need for other types of expertise around the enterprise-wide risk management system. Indeed this may be a very sensible approach although it does not appear quite consistent with the ERM principle of full integration.

In Carlsberg's case the development of a unique strategic risk management approach was championed by an individual outside the official risk management function—an experienced professional that headed the Internal Audit function at the time. We also note that this individual relocated after the change in top management whereafter strategic risk management became an integrated part of the traditional risk management function.[13] This case does not conclude with a stark lesson. It is unclear whether the enterprise-wide integration of risk management actually materialized, but a reason for skepticism might be the changes in new executive risk management roles that could slow the integration process. Even if integration was achieved, there is no evidence that it resulted in a better handling of Group strategic risks. While it is impossible to draw a firm conclusion here, we see an illustration of how ERM can be subjected to change in spite of its performance.

GENERAL MILLS

General Mills has been long noted for its commitment to good corporate governance.[14] The Audit Committee oversees internal controls, financial reporting, legal compliance, and ERM. The company has had an ERM process in place since the late 2000s, although according to observers it had become 'ripe for a revamp'—needing better risk mitigation follow-ups and alignment with strategic planning.[15] In part, this could be reflected in the past pursuit of a high dividend yield policy that made the stock popular among investors in the low interest-rate environment. However, this policy also caused an erosion in innovation with falling market shares and declining profits in contrast to the lofty aspirations.[16] It appears the ERM process was mostly applied for financial, economic, and operational risk assessments while strategic risk factors that could affect the long-term viability of the enterprise seemed to be disregarded.

A critical event in this short case occurred when the company's leading Yoplait yogurt brand fell behind Chobani and Danone with sales plunging in excess of 20% during 2016 (after dropping more than 5% the year before). While the company has a number of strong food brands in its portfolio including Cheerios, Wheaties, Pillsbury, Old El Paso and Häagen-Dazs—Yoplait counted for almost a fifth of corporate revenues. Obviously, the deteriorating yogurt sales was a wake-up call. What seems obvious to observers is that General Mills was late in responding to Chobani's introduction of Greek yogurts and ended up playing catch-up—with mixed results.[17] Putting this situation into a risk management frame, we might say that strategic risks did not seem to figure squarely at the center of the ERM process. To be fair, managing strategic risks is a very difficult and demanding order.

So, despite having an ERM process in place, General Mills missed the high impact competitive developments in the important yogurt market. Whereas the ERM process appeared to provide detailed reporting on financial and economic exposures with advanced Value-at-Risk monitoring, it was not able to identify the biggest risks embedded in the competitive market dynamic.

Various initiatives have been taken in the interim to introduce new products across the spectrum of cereals and power bars to new yogurt types with lower levels of sweetener to boost sales growth. We (and others) would observe that these efforts may also increase the cost of more complex product lines that put pressure on future profit margins and net earnings. That is, the expansion through new product offerings is not without risk either.[18]

Let us be fair and report that new risk management approaches considered by the Audit Committee seem to promise more leadership engagement, use of advanced data analytics, and adoption of a risk appetite statement to foster more risk-taking activities.[19] However, we offer one quibble here that suggests a future discussion. Can these new measures be successfully adopted and integrated into overall management thinking? In other words, our concern is less on the efficacy of the measures taken and more on the use of those measures by management. As noted in previous and coming chapters, human behavior—not systems and processes—tends to lie under most risk management issues.[20]

A final note. As things are, US companies with assets in excess of $10 million and shares held by more than 2,000 owners must file annual reports with the SEC (Securities and Exchange Commission) disclosed on a Form 10-K and consider new emergent risks that may affect the business. In other words, when General Mills and other larger companies have to identify and define major strategic risks, we are probably witnessing the consequence of a legal reporting requirement rather than the outcomes of conscious strategic risk management processes and thinking.

WELL THEN, DOES ERM ACTUALLY PAY OFF?

Set aside the compare-and-contrast discussion that so far has dominated this chapter. What evidence do we have to support one view or another?

Here we revisit the potentially existential problem with ERM (or any risk management framework for that matter). That is, despite the strong promotion of formal ERM frameworks as the proper approach to deal with major corporate risks, there actually is little empirical evidence to support those claims. Or, at least the accumulated results so far are inconclusive with respect to the ultimate effects. As discussed previously, various institutions began advocating a holistic integrated approach to internal control and risk management in the 1990s (e.g., COSO, 1992, 1996) that had developed into systematic ERM frameworks by the turn of the millennium (e.g., COSO, 2004; ISO, 2009). The idea was that the integrated treatment of different risks through the coordination effort of a central corporate function, say a Risk Office, rather than being dealt with by departmental silos, would provide more effective handling of interrelated risks across business activities.[21]

Adopting risk-adjusted return requirements in major investment decisions should ensure that optimal amounts of risk are being assigned to projects that achieve the intended earnings targets within acceptable levels of default. This view is consistent with a guiding 'risk appetite' approach, where the idea is that top management and the board can express the proper risk levels in advance as a guide to subsequent business decisions made in different parts of the organization. This also carries with it the idea that only non-core business exposures should be hedged using insurance, or derivative markets, whereas the organization should assume more risk within its core business where it is supposed to have strong managerial capabilities and thereby gaining a so-called 'comparative advantage in risk-bearing.'[22]

However, the empirical studies do not universally confirm that the proposed benefits actually materialize.

To be as clear as we can here, the empirical evidence we presently have available on the motivation for implementing ERM and the ensuing performance effects from the implemented practices remains rather uncertain. Research has found that ERM typically is associated with high financial leverage, or gearing of balance sheets, the size of the firm, and direct board involvement.[23] Some studies do not find any effect of ERM on the company stock price or on corporate performance outcomes.[24] Other studies find that ERM is associated with higher operating profit, efficiency measures, and revenue generation.[25] However, taken together these results are rather equivocal.

This is obviously disturbing given the prominent stature and position ERM has assumed among business opinionators, regulators, and public policy-makers. Yet, there is a ray of sunshine. A recent study does find that adherence to the *principles* outlined by the major ERM frameworks can have positive performance effects, particularly when the associated risk management practices are channeled through or fed into the strategic planning process of the organization.[26]

This finding means that firms can adhere to the principles of ERM (since they are spelled out in the referenced study, rather than being equated to the application of an ERM framework) without actually having anything like formal ERM practices implemented in the organization. In other words, it suggests that it is not the implementation of something people refer to as equivalent to a formal ERM framework that matters. What makes the difference is how you *think* and what you *do* in the organization and how you manage your business possibly supported by ERM ideas. So, implementing an ERM framework is not a panacea that can resolve all risk management challenges for an organization. But, it can make a difference *how* the framework is being used and applied within the organization.

This brings us back to the earlier stated proposition, that good and effective risk managers might be just that. They are good managers of risk, but they do not necessarily deploy anything like an ERM framework in the organization, although they obviously also could have that, if they can use it to their advantage. This leads us to a preliminary conclusion that adoption of ERM is neither a necessary nor sufficient condition for developing effective risk management capabilities that can generate superior risk management and performance outcomes. Dare we insert the observation here that what does seem to matter is human behavior, values, culture, and critical thinking as the fundamental influences on the chances for risk management effectiveness?

I do as I do, not as you say

Here we enter a critical moment in our central argument, which is that the way in which actual risk management practices are being executed in organizations is notably different from the espoused practices promoted by the formal ERM frameworks—and that understanding this fact tells us something beyond the difficulty of implementing organization-wide change. Furthermore, there is a question as to whether conformance with ERM frameworks reflects a social urge rather than actually delivering on the expected outcomes (recalling Jane Austen's quote here).

We can state a more technical interpretation of our view in the following two points:

1. The predominating view of risk management today is governed by its history, beginning as a collection of technical functions, which themselves were developed to address risks (measurable uncertainties), thus leading to a foundational assumption that risk management primarily is about accumulating sufficient quantitative data on threats to the organization in order to take measures to mitigate potential impacts. This statement, we believe, anchors the generally accepted current view in the business world. Some may push back that a lot of innovations have been added. For example— among other adjustments and extensions—a view is emerging rapidly that risk management should apply to opportunity management as well as threat management. The recent 'standardization' movement has advanced an integrated framework of external expectations into the risk management story.

   However, there are two things to say about that. First, the narrative of this story is not the result of a rational, critically analyzed, step-by-step progression, but is the result of a series of contingent events, decisions, responses, and pure happenstance. Probably for the reason of 'path dependency' the end result reinforces the underlying foundation of risk management as a largely reactive effort to mitigate threats. And second, even new developments and innovations are still presented and discussed *in relation* to the historical foundation—we might think of this effect as similar to adding an extension to a house, rather than building a new house.

2. Yes, COSO/ISO imagine that each organization will develop ERM in a manner consistent with the organizational context, and thus risk management will look different from organization to organization. But at the same time the standardization movement seeks to present a framework that contains certain core elements. While perhaps not intending to do so, the drivers of the standardization movement have thereby created something of a paradox. All organizations will have a different approach to risk management, but here is a guideline for what risk management should look like to make the advantages come true.

   We want to be very careful here, in stating the following. It is quite plausible to interpret the preceding statement as: While risk management is likely to differ across organizations, organizations may desire some guidance in beginning to introduce ERM. Yet, our final two chapters will attempt to establish that the more appropriate reading of this statement is: Yes, we really should think very carefully about how uncertainty affects our organization and then develop the organizational-specific means to assess and address that uncertainty, but—really—it is much easier to follow guidelines.

There is our trouble in a nutshell. The gravitational pull of the history of risk management almost invariably pulls us into the traditional way of thinking. And when we try to adjust to accommodate additional new ways of thinking, we further limit our ability to step back and truly examine the question of what risk management really *is*. We are pretty solid on what risk management *can do*—tools, techniques, methods, and models—but what is it? We will construct an answer that rests on a progression of eight underlying statements:

> Statement One: The central focus of risk management has been *risk*, but the primary focus should be on *uncertainty*, and this reorientation will become increasingly emphasized as the business environment becomes both more dynamic and complex, and where potential risk events are hard to foresee and their true effects unpredictable.
> Statement Two: It can be argued that risk is an objective phenomenon (by 'objective' is meant that independent observations will yield consistent results ... it will rain tomorrow or it will not rain tomorrow), but *risk* and *uncertainty* are nonetheless fundamentally mental constructs.
> Statement Three: Because *risk* and *uncertainty* are mental constructs, it would seem essential that risk management must rest on an understanding of human behavior under conditions of uncertainty.

<u>Statement Four</u>: Because *risk* and *uncertainty* are mental constructs, it would seem to be crucial that risk management also focuses critical attention on the role of culture as shaping perceptions.

<u>Statement Five</u>: Because *risk* and *uncertainty* are mental constructs, it would seem to be crucial that risk management focuses critical attention on how the values embedded in the culture shape perceptions and hence responses to risk and uncertainty.

<u>Statement Six</u>: Owing to Statements One to Five, organizations and managers encounter a particular struggle to incorporate long-run perspectives into the enactment of organizational actions, although the long-run effects are essential aspects of risk management.

<u>Statement Seven</u>: Owing to Statements One to Six, effective risk management outcomes are contingent upon everything that goes on within the organization, i.e., risk management is everything.

<u>Statement Eight</u>: Owing to Statements One to Seven, effective risk management requires continuous critical thinking among individuals in all areas and at all levels of the organization, i.e., risk management is fundamentally a way of engaging in critical thinking.

A POST-SCRIPT ... SOMETHING TO THINK ABOUT

The responsibility for risk management and internal controls in the Vestas Group (a global manufacturer of wind turbines) rested with the Board of Directors and subsequently the Executive Committee constituted by a two-person team: Ditlev Engel, President and CEO, and Henrik Nørremark, Deputy CEO, Chief Operating Officer (COO), and acting Chief Financial Officer (CFO). The company officially emphasized good risk management and internal controls to minimize the risk of errors in international operations and it worked diligently to improve its risk management system. The risk management process was continuously identifying, assessing, and addressing key risks to reduce the financial impact from those risks. The ERM processes were integrated across all business units adopting a standardized approach to manage Group risks, which—the firm argued—had enabled significant reductions in insurance premiums.

The integrated risk management function was performed by a dedicated office, headed by a Group Risk Manager as part of the Finance area reporting to the Group CFO, Henrik Nørremark. Hence, the Finance function was instrumental in forming the risk management process and ensuring that systematic identification and handling of all relevant risks was carried out. The Board of Directors and the Executive Committee would—as explicitly stated—assess potential risks of fraud twice a year. The implementation of risk management and internal controls was officially done to ensure compliance with strategic aims, corporate policies, and procedures. In sum, Vestas presented the outside world with a well-structured ERM approach to identify, assess, and monitor major risks from a central Risk Office.

The CEO, Ditlev Engel, was appointed to lead the Vestas Group in 2005 when the company was challenged by unsatisfactory quality components from external suppliers in a supply chain that was stretched by the international reach of the firm. Mr. Engel successfully addressed this by investing heavily to internationalize the production forging ahead in a quest to gain global market share. As a consequence the business grew, profits soared, and the stock price went to an all-time peak in 2007 earning Engel the title of 'Mr. Wind Power.'

Given the global structure of the Vestas Group much emphasis was given to improve operational performance and minimize potential operational disruptions, e.g., by collaborating with suppliers and integrating product development with customers, sales, and production units to reduce lead times and lower costs. However, the global financial crisis of 2008 hit the international demand for investments in wind-generating hardware. Customers were unable to secure funding for long-term energy infrastructure projects and the order book began to shrink rapidly. The global expansion strategy yielded negative effects on the Group financial performance and the stock price nearly halved between 2008 and 2011.

Ditlev Engel continued to follow the initial strategic path laid out in 2005 despite the dramatic changes in global business conditions in the wake of the financial crisis in 2008 and even with clear signs in 2010 that his (in)action had serious and impactful consequences for the financial performance. Why this strategy was retained remains a mystery since, in hindsight, it seems quite obvious that such dramatic changes in market conditions would call for major adjustments.

This phenomenon, we believe, may be ascribed to the difficulty of dealing with unexpected events that defeat simple linear projections of the past, or maybe a determined adherence to the given path as an effect of overconfidence created by previous successes. It also might be influenced by an ERM framework with the stated purpose of ensuring that prior strategic targets and objectives are achieved, come what may. And, it might also reflect what some researchers refer to as a *prior hypothesis bias*, in which a decision-maker tends to overestimate the importance of information that confirms her/his beliefs and undervalue or discard contradictory information.[27] Another term for this is *confirmation bias*, referenced in the opening passages of this chapter.

In any event, no adaptive changes were made, and performance showed signs of continued deterioration. While Engel had been awarded stock options, all the options were deeply out-of-the-money. Hence, we speculate whether he suffered from a form of *escalating commitment bias*. This phenomenon is often observed among financial traders; that is, a person continues to increase a position based on a strong belief, or interest in a market price increase, even though the market continues to move in a negative direction.

The Board became nervous and did attempt to fire Engel in 2011. For various reasons that probably will remain hidden to the public due to internal confidentiality limitations, the Board did not succeed at first and then an unusual chain of events unfolded.

The CFO, Henrik Nørremark, was accused of defrauding the Vestas Group for around US$20 million linked to transactions with an Indian business partner. The Board fired Nørremark in February 2012 after he had held the CFO position for eight years. With his departure, the head of the Risk Office was also discharged and the ERM process no longer had either a Risk Manager or a responsible Risk Leader. Given the bi-annual focus by the Board and Executive Committee on the potential for fraudulent acts in the Vestas Group, this whole set of affairs seemed to set Vestas on a precarious path.

It came to light that CEO Engel and the Board claimed that the Indian business deals had been transacted without due authorization and without their knowledge, and this was the basis for Engel's recommendation that the Board fire Nørremark. These events appear to have served as a distraction buying Engel additional time as CEO. He was not officially fired by the Board until August 2013—by that time receiving a separation compensation of two years' salary. Interestingly, Nørremark was never convicted and his case has since been withdrawn. Further, in 2017, Henrik Nørremark was awarded a total compensation of around US$7 million in a secret settlement with the Vestas Group partly as compensation for the firing.

So, here we have the implementation of a formal ERM framework supported in all the right ways, but which through intriguing maneuvers at the very highest governance level was unable to deliver much in terms of safeguarding the company against the biggest strategic risks—including poor decisions at the highest levels of an organization. The exposure to a doomed strategic course heading toward disaster was allowed to continue without anyone being able to challenge the direction, including the risk management function itself, which was sacrificed by the CEO and the Board as a response that seems mystifying, but which bore all the hallmarks of scapegoating.

In a later development, Engel was ultimately replaced by Anders Runevad as CEO (in August 2013). He revised the corporate strategy and returned the company to profitability the following year. The risk management process was revived and a highly regarded Enterprise Risk Manager was appointed to lead these activities. The integrated Group-wide enterprise risk management framework was revamped with a continued focus on risk identification, evaluation, treatment, monitoring, and quarterly reporting for discussions in the Group Risk Management Committee counting various senior managers and chaired by the CFO. In other words, the new leadership team implemented a restructured ERM system to support the management and governance of the Vestas Group going forward.

This train of events offers an opportunity for reflection:

1. Should the ERM process have detected and addressed the rapid deterioration of the market and the adverse economic developments in 2008? And, what actually could have been done?
2. What exactly was the Risk Manager's involvement in the process and was his firing (as well as that of the CFO, the official Risk Leader) symbolic/sacrificial or legitimate?
3. How (or) can ERM become sufficiently self-aware of its own conduct and cognizant about the potential adverse impact of flawed practices?

As appears, this whole true story is infused with moral issues and behavioral concerns that deserve much more attention. We turn to these issues in Chapter 4.

NOTES

1   Austen, J. (1811). *Sense and Sensibility*. Thomas Edgerton Publishing. London. Jane Austen (1775–1817) is primarily known for her novels that capture the values of English landowners where marriage typically was used as the means to obtain economic safety and gain in social stature.
2   See, for example, Henriksen, Per (2018). *Enterprise Risk Management: Rationaler og Paradokser i en Moderne Ledelsesteknologi*. PhD Dissertation, Doctoral School of Business and Management, Copenhagen Business School.
3   The concept of risk leadership (and the associated term, Risk Leader, has emerged in a rather organic unsystematic fashion where the central organizing concept remains a bit elusive. We hope to add some clarity, but here offer two representative illustrations of how the term is used elsewhere: Stephanson, C. (2010). The role of leadership in risk management. *Ivy Business Journal* (Nov/ Dec); and From risk management to risk leadership: A conversation with David O. Renz (2017). *The Nonprofit Quarterly*.

4   University of St. Thomas (2013). *The Risk Leadership Challenge: Final Report.* UST Press.

5   E.g., Paul L. Walker and William G. Shenkir (2008). Implementing Enterprise Risk Management. *Journal of Accountancy*, March 1.

6   E.g., Carol Fox (2012). Ten Easy Steps to Implement Enterprise Risk Management, November 14 [a *presentation at the 2012 RIMS Annual Conference in Philadelphia*].

7   The Carlsberg Group website https://carlsberggroup.com/who-we-are/corporate-governance/auditing-internal-control-risk-management/.

8   Vibeke Aggerholm (2013). Risk management: Approach and methodology in Carlsberg, Henry Stewart Talks.

9   The Carlsberg Group Annual Report 2015.

10   John Kell (2015). Carlsberg taps first non-Danish CEO in beer maker's 168-year history, *Fortune*, February 18. http://fortune.com/2015/02/18/carlsberg-first-non-dane-ceo/. Christina Zander (2015). Carlsberg to replace CEO: Cut costs as profit falls—Danish brewer hurt by weakening Russian ruble, *Wall Street Journal*, February 18. www.wsj.com/articles/carlsberg-to-replace-ceo-cut-costs-as-profit-falls-1424251115.

11   Today Vibeke Aggerholm is the Chief Risk Officer of Copenhagen Infrastructure Partners.

12   The Carlsberg Group Annual Report 2017.

13   General Mills, Corporate Governance Principles, September 24, 2018. https://investors.generalmills.com/corporate-governance/governance-documents/default.aspx.

14   Fresh insights from the Spring 2018 NCSU ERM Roundtable Summit. https://erm.ncsu.edu/library/article/fresh-insights-from-the-spring-2018-ncsu-erm-roundtable-summit.

15   David Kolpak (2016). General Mills: The risks run deeper than its sky-high valuation, August 24. https://seekingalpha.com/article/4001886-general-mills-risks-run-deeper-sky-high-valuation.

16   John Kell (2017). General Mills loses the culture wars. May 22 (in the June 1, 2017 issue of *Fortune*). http://fortune.com/2017/05/22/general-mills-yoplait-greek-yogurt/.

17   Michelle Lodge (2018). General Mills' plans to emphasize sales growth carry risks: Packaged goods giant counting on new cereals, energy bars and yogurt to boost sales. Jul 11, *TheStreet*. www.thestreet.com/investing/general-mills-plans-to-emphasize-sales-carry-risks-14648218.

18   Leading Practices in Enterprise Risk Management, ViewPoints, Audit Committee Leadership Network, April, 2015. www.ey.com/Publication/vwLUAssets/EY-viewpoints-leading-practices-in-enterprise-risk-management/$FILE/EY-viewpoints-leading-practices-in-enterprise-risk-management.pdf.

19   General Mills, Annual Report 2018.

20   Arena, M., Arnaboldi, M. and Azzone, G. (2010). The organizational dynamics of enterprise risk management. *Accounting, Organizations and Society*, 35: 659–675. Barton, T.L., Shenkir, W.G. and Walker, P. L. (2002). *Making Enterprise Risk Management Pay Off*. Financial Times/Prentice Hall, Upper Saddle River, NJ. Dickinson, G. (2001). Enterprise risk management: Its origins and conceptual foundation. *The Geneva Papers on Risk and Insurance*, 26: 360–366. Olson, D.L. and Wu, D.D. (2008). *Enterprise Risk Management* (2nd ed.). Singapore: World Scientific.

21   Nocco, B.W. and Stulz, R.M. (2006). Enterprise Risk Management: Theory and Practice. *Journal of Applied Corporate Finance*, 18(4): 8–20.

22   Beasley, M.S., Clune, R. and Hermanson, D.R. (2005). Enterprise risk management: An empirical analysis of factors associated with the extent of

implementation. *Journal of Accounting and Public Policy*, 24: 521–531. Gordon, L.A., Loeb, M.P. and Tseng, C. (2009). Enterprise risk management and firm performance: A contingency perspective. *Journal of Accounting and Public Policy*, 28: 301–327. Liebenberg, A.P. and Hoyt, R.E. (2003). The determinants of enterprise risk management: Evidence from the appointment of Chief Risk Officers. *Risk Management and Insurance Review*, 6: 37–52. Pagach, D. and Warr, R. (2011). The characteristics of firms that hire Chief Risk Officers. *Journal of Risk and Insurance*, 78: 185–211.

23　Beasley, M.S., Pagach, D. and Warr, R. (2008). Information conveyed in hiring announcements of senior executives overseeing enterprise-wide risk management processes. *Journal of Accounting, Auditing and Finance*, 23: 311–332. Quon, T.K., Zeghal, D. and.Maingot, M. (2012). Enterprise risk management and firm performance. *Procedia—Social and Behavioral Sciences*, 62: 263–267.

24　Eckles, D.L., Hoyt, R.E. and Miller, S.M. (2014). The impact of enterprise risk management on the marginal cost of reducing risk: Evidence from the insurance industry. *Journal of Banking and Finance*, 43: 247–261. Grace, M.F., Leverty, J.T., Phillips, R.D. and Shimpi, P. (2015) The value of investing in Enterprise Risk Management. *Journal of Risk and Insurance*, 82: 289–316.

25　E.g., Schwenk, C.R. (1984). Cognitive simplification processes in strategic decision-making. *Strategic Management Journal*, 5(2): 111–128.

4 Thinking about (thinking about) risk management

One of the painful things about our time is that those who feel certainty are stupid, and those with any imagination and understanding are filled with doubt and indecision.

Bertrand Russell[1]

An 'and yet ...' seems to be missing from the end of Russell's quotation. Our inclination obviously is not to side with stupidity, but neither are we promoting indecision as a managerial posture. Nevertheless, Russell strikes near enough to the sensibility we are trying to capture. We think the point here is to recognize that particularly significant troubles in life and work arise when we are absolutely certain an outcome will obtain. Trouble also comes from indecision, as we will see in this chapter, but the central risks arising from human perception and thinking tend toward overconfidence and much less often to indecision as a general rule. There are reasons we believe this is true in organizations, but mainly that is because top-level managers are, anyway, individuals rarely lacking in self-confidence.

Never say *never* and never say *always* is sage risk management advice, so let us soften the edges of the opening quotation. A key feature of imagination—to use Russell's word—is not indecision but skepticism. For example, certain future prospects in some objective sense might approach near certainty but being conscious of flaws in our ability to perceive and think should always be embedded in our decision-making processes. We should consider alternative outcomes, likelihoods, why we might be wrong, and—well—we must rely on critical thinking.

We turn our attention more fully to the idea that risk management is a way of conducting, accommodating, or facilitating critical thinking. In the course of doing this, we first attempt to sharpen the general argument, and then we delve into the human dimension of risk management; how we as humans perceive our uncertain world, factors that influence that perception, and associated issues that are critical to risk management. Along the way we will include a number of short stories that illustrate particular points we want to raise about the centrality of the *human factor* in risk management.

SETTING THE STAGE

Our previous chapters laid out how the formal enterprise risk management (ERM) frameworks have emerged over time in order to discuss what can actually be observed in real organizations that aspire to implement and use the formal ERM guidelines. Arising from this discussion we make two key observations: 1) espoused ERM and ERM in practice are not aligned—partly for developmental reasons but also, we believe, for having gotten the true nature of risk management the 'wrong way around,' and 2) the evidence that ERM contributes unequivocally to organizational value-adding efforts is inconsistent to nonexistent.

Chapter 3's discussion speaks for itself, but we would like to pick up and examine a particular insight revealed there. Over the history of risk management, a specific dynamic has emerged that emphasizes a strengthening of the internal reporting and control perspectives as essential remedies for adopting the ERM frameworks. We saw evidence of this in the wake of the major corporate scandals around Enron, Parmelat, Tyco International, and Worldcom that led to the Sarbanes-Oxley legislation in 2002. Yet, despite these efforts there were subsequent examples of Sarbanes-Oxley compliant institutions that nonetheless continued to fail, e.g., Société Générale where a so-called rogue trader, Jérôme Kerviel, was able to vastly exceed his risk limits—an action that eventually cost the bank around €5 billion to unwind. By the way, there is also research evidence indicating that necessary risk-taking innovation suffered as a consequence of this legislation, resulting in a reduced capacity to find better and more creative solutions to deal with an uncertain future.[2]

This might be a somewhat harsh verdict, but it is nevertheless true that the Sarbanes-Oxley restrictions were unable to prevent a major financial and economic crisis from occurring in 2008. This time the financial sector overextended itself in a lemming-like drive to become excessively exposed in a deeply complex (complex, that is, by the sector's own design) sub-prime loan market. Arriving at this result required a nearly industry-wide commitment to convert junk-quality sub-prime loans into portfolios of investment grade securities through the manipulation of derivative instruments and attendant 'white-washing' by rating agencies. There is obviously additional insight to be gained by noting that many key advisors earned sizable intermediation and advisory fees along the way.

The climatic conditions led everyone (the lemmings), with a few notable exceptions, toward a free fall down the cliffs in pursuit of maximizing their own and their shareholders' wealth. Many institutions in the financial markets engaged in copycat behavior, which seemed to legitimize the decisions and permitting—not to put too fine a point on it—institutions to not have to *think* too much about what they were doing. Some probably felt they had to do the same as everyone else for competitive reasons, because good money was made from it (at least at the time), and underperformance might lead to ridicule in the board room. We humbly submit that this partially illuminates our central thesis. Risk management is not about doing things on a whim, or doing what everybody else is doing (even if it is profitable), or doing slavishly what is prescribed in a formal set of guidelines. It is about *thinking*—that is engaging in critical thinking.

Much was learned from the financial crisis. For example it was *not* as much a technical breakdown of risk management and control processes as it was a failure of mass perception regarding proper exposures in the financial sector driven by major cognitive biases among key decision makers. Oh yes, and it was partially motivated by self-interest as well. To this is added an obvious link to moral and/or ethical issues of proper, or improper behaviors among decision-makers in the executive echelons. So, the market collapse seemed more linked to failures in organizational cultures and ethics than anything else, which—to be fair—has, indeed, fostered some self-reflection and soul searching in the aftermath.[3]

However, time has marched on and lessons learned have faded into the past (*forgetting* is a source of cognitive risk or uncertainty). Consequently, the emphasis has now returned to the old focus on risk controls and more stringent reporting requirements—not least in the financial sector, where we have seen the argument prevail that the major cause of the financial crisis was insufficient control processes and reporting to support and guide the governance of corporate risk. So, back on the same old horse—back to the control-based view that served as a foundation for the original ERM framing. And this despite evidence that the boards among those banks that were hardest hit from the crisis, in fact, took conscious decisions to increase exposures—motivated as they were (officially at least) to optimize the returns for shareholders.[4]

We also are presently seeing arguments that those systems and controls should be rolled back to foster (in the extreme) entirely free unregulated financial markets. This is not our view, if that should appear to be the case. That argument is based on the idea that the markets will 'regulate' good and bad behavior, and we do not see much evidence that this happens either. It could be said that fully free-market proponents see the problem as human behavior, and we do too. However, the idea that the market will somehow control for bad behavior would—in our judgment—set Adam Smith spinning in his grave.[5, 6]

A RESTATEMENT

We believe there are six fundamental issues with the current views of the risk management guidelines, and each of these issues, we argue, contributes to the observed distance between espoused and actual practices:

1. Guidelines largely ignore the human dimension of risk management.
2. Guidelines do not focus adequately on the uncertain and the unknowable.
3. Despite recent proclamations to the contrary, risk management remains oriented toward measurable uncertainty and threat management.
4. Leadership in response to risk and uncertainty is not addressed in any meaningful way.
5. Guidelines do not reflect how humans can/should 'work' collaboratively (or not).
6. Guidelines largely presume that coordination and integration are unalloyed value-adding features of risk management.

This itemization may not precisely clarify the underlying description of the disconnections, so, we offer a tentative attempt to consolidate them:

> A fundamental problem with current guidelines for risk management in organizations is that they do not reflect a basic understanding of the centrality of human nature, the way humans interact, and the way humans 'encounter' or perceive the world in assessing and addressing risk and uncertainty. Within that general critique is a prominent specific challenge, that current guidelines for risk management do not consider the context of some of the major emergent risks, critical uncertainties, and unpredictable/unforeseeable phenomena.

Let us briefly elaborate on this statement by emphasizing that the mechanical or technical aspects of risk management are not being critiqued here. As noted earlier, the things we do to assess and address risks are—commonly—highly beneficial, unless of course they over time turn into routinized bureaucratic reporting rituals, which in turn literally stop people from *thinking*. Through these measures fewer people are injured on the job, fewer defective products make their way into the marketplace, duplication strategies limit the chance of total losses from a single event, seatbelts reduce the frequency of driver deaths, and so on. No, we are not challenging the efficacy of the risk management tools. However, while we are on the subject of risk management tool implementation, there is something we should note.

One of the under-represented topics in traditional risk management discussions is the failure to fully reflect how humans view and interpret the risk management measures themselves (heat maps, Value-at-Risk methods, limits and caps, risk appetite, as well as more prosaic tools like loss prevention and reduction applications). Put as simply as possible, the risk management measures we adopt might themselves be a source of risk and uncertainty for the organizations that use them. The introduction of a risk management application might change the risk, or migrate the risk to a new location, or in extreme situations, even make the risk worse. The subject of moral hazard (that is, the introduction of changes in behavior as the result of a risk management tool) does receive attention in the risk management and insurance academic literatures, but it rarely receives the full-bore attention it deserves as a matter of practical managerial decision-making. Take just a few illustrative examples:

- Safer highways encourage drivers to speed.
- The presence of kidnap and ransom insurance may actually promote kidnapping.
- Saving money through reduced accident frequency reduces risk management budget allocations for subsequent years.
- Health care costs may migrate from group health programs to workers' compensation if there is a sufficient differential in the benefit, costs, or limitations under the two programs.
- Introducing closed circuit cameras may cause crime to migrate to other locations.

We could go on here, but in each instance the risk management issue here is people, leadership, and reflexive behaviors. Adopting or imposing particular risk management measures can change behavior for the better (incentives to stop smoking), but also for the worse. This means that behavior is not a secondary matter in risk management, it is *the* central issue.

But, let us get back to the subject at hand. It is our impression that current ERM approaches primarily focus on the 'doing of things,' and only secondarily pay attention to the people who are expected to do or respond to those things. Organizations are social systems where individuals act and interact in complex ways, and the dynamics of these complex systems will have a significant influence on realized outcomes. We expect some push-back on this assertion of the risk management process, so we want to be as clear as possible. Hence, in our view, the following points prevail:

First, the central fact in understanding risk management is that our world is fundamentally constituted of uncertainties (and the unknown). Risk management is then a misleading term: Uncertainty management is actually more appropriate—although later we will even wonder about the sufficiency of that term.

Second, we, as humans, very much desire a world of measurable uncertainty, and indeed are determined to promote the seeking of a firmer, more quantitative, understanding of our uncertain world. But, by framing our field as—in the first instance—a matter of assessing and addressing risks we would argue that we thereby mis-specify what managers actually do, and this further places assumptions and expectations that can prove to be harmful. Certainly, it is fair to say that massive resources have been expended by organizations to refine the measurement of risks. We wonder whether some of these resources might be better spent on understanding the human nature and the behavior of individuals in social systems under conditions of uncertainty.

Third, human nature and behavior are central subjects of interest in risk management. They are the 'what' and 'why' of our field. Historically risk management has been framed as addressing the 'how.' How is important too—no doubt—but how is an expression of the what and why, so it is a second order issue.

Fourth, human nature and behavior are inextricably entwined with moral and ethical considerations and the values held by individual organizational actors, in a very real sense, will influence the first line response to emergent risk, uncertainty, and unknowability. The values, beliefs, and behaviors of people will shape the organizational risk management responses, but we might even go so far as to say that our/ their values *are* risk management. They guide our thinking and the subsequent responses in uncertain and unfamiliar situations.

While waiting to spell this out until the final chapter, the above points imply that a functioning risk manager/leader needs to know particular things that historically have not been part of the recognized knowledge, skills, and abilities ascribed to the risk management field.

Before moving on with the subject of humans and human behavior, we want to reinforce our argument through a set of illustrative stories. So, consider the following corporate examples:

> **Lehman Brothers**—the international investment bank—is an example of a highly successful global securities firm that, according to its own annual reports, was using state-of-the-art risk management tools and approaches to monitor and control its diverse business activities. Yet, the official records report that its financial exposures were consciously and deliberately increasing, reflecting the bank's extended engagement into various subprime loan investment vehicles.[6] So, even if it well may be argued that the techniques supporting the VaR calculations were potentially flawed, or imprecise, the officially reported VaR measures clearly indicated to everyone (including the board) that Lehman Brothers continued to increase their subprime exposure right until the moment of the crisis. They also had a top management in place that ousted those people who warned against the excessive exposures along the way.[7] In fact, this action was led by a CEO (incidentally among the ten highest paid executives in the US) who was secured a sizeable bonus only months before the firm collapsed, an event now reckoned to be a key trigger of the 2008 financial crisis.

This seems to reflect risk management behaviors in practice that (probably consciously) were inconsistent with the practices espoused in the annual report and other official documents. This is what Mitroff and Silvers refer to as Type 4 errors—the worst category—where decision-makers intentionally try to mislead others to commit or legitimize commitment of Type 1, 2, or 3 errors.[8] This obviously has ethical undertones reflected in a leadership style driven by extreme self-interest at the expense of other stakeholders, e.g., employees, shareholders/owners, and society, and exhibiting common leadership flaws and psychological biases. These leadership traits clearly display some of the bad habits of spectacularly unsuccessful people identified by Professor Sydney Finkelstein, e.g., they believe they dominate their surroundings, think they have all the right answers, eliminate anyone who is not in full agreement, and fail to distinguish between personal and corporate interests.[9]

> **Nokia**—the once dominant global mobile phone producer explained in the annual reports running up to 2007 how it applied ERM. The company adhered to sound risk management principles, e.g., using derivatives for hedging and calculating VaR to assess corporate exposures with regular exposure reports to the board. The stated

purpose was to identify financial, operational, and strategic risks that might prevent Nokia from reaching its business objectives. It was also noted that everyone in the organization was responsible for identifying significant risks. Yet, top management was unable to see in time the emerging relevance and impending market potential of smartphones and instead continued to focus on cheap sturdy mobile phones for the large emerging markets. This 'bottom of the pyramid' mass market perspective received a lot of attention and was a popular fad at the time.[10] The company was very successful in this endeavor and the Nokia phones still to this day have many supporters because the phones simply continue to work—they were durable high-quality products. This is possibly in contrast to the smartphones that (it seems) only are expected to have a lifetime of five years, or less. However, in the process senior management completely overlooked the threat from Apple's interconnected iPhone despite having thousands of highly skilled development engineers in the organization and many enabling technologies ready for application. So, in this case the adopted ERM approach was unable to identify and deal with *the* biggest risk—Apple—that eventually brought the established world dominance of Nokia mobile phones to a complete halt.[11]

In many ways, this story resembles other accounts of successful dominant companies that failed to renew the business activities and adapt their market position to fit the changing customer demands, technologies, or competitive moves. Eastman Kodak's failure to advance into digital photography—a technology the company had invented itself—is a much used example of this phenomenon. The common explanation is that prior success blinded top management so they failed to see the new market opportunities where a more balanced view is that you also need to master and organize the capabilities needed to develop a new (or renew the existing) business.[12]

What is so interesting about Nokia is that the company had all the technologies, capabilities, people, and skills required to develop a state of the art smartphone but failed to orchestrate it all and bring it to market. And, of course note here that top management and the board had put in place an ERM system with the purpose of safeguarding against unforeseen risks—precisely so as not to be taken by surprise. However, what happened was seemingly the opposite, that ERM provided a false sense of security by focusing attention on those risks that could be identified and measured, but lost sight of those *big* hard-to-quantify risks that could severely damage Nokia's core business—mobile phones.

Telia Sonera—the Swedish-based international telecom provider had implemented risk management as an integral part of the business control and monitoring processes with the stated intent of identifying risks and circumventing potential effects that could materially affect the ability to achieve their objectives. Yet, this risk management approach did not prevent senior people in the organization from paying bribes to an Uzbek government official to ease the acquisition of a local operator, Coscom, in Uzbekistan in 2007 in pursuit of the strategic goal to expand and dominate the Eurasian market. The incident, which was only discovered later, was eventually settled with US$1 billion fines paid to the US, Swedish, and Dutch authorities.[13] These transactions obviously took place with the implicit knowledge of senior executives and, maybe for that reason, allowed the practices to evade the radar of the formal ERM process. That is an unproven speculation. Nonetheless, the chief executive of TeliaSonera was subsequently forced to resign in February 2014.

Whatever the specific circumstances, this provides another example of ERM not doing the job despite using the proclaimed tools and processes advanced by the usual supportive argumentation to justify its implementation. As another curious aspect, it highlights the ethical dimensions often observed among the corporate leadership when a major risk event occurs. The case illustrates how a formal ERM framework may be a quite effective risk control mechanism when dealing with smaller financial and operational transactions and incidents but has difficulty dealing with non-standardized high-level business decisions—particularly involving senior managers. As observed in other cases the ethical habits of senior management play a crucial role here as do the core values and behaviors of organizational members in general.

Telenor—the multinational Norwegian telecommunication company—implemented a risk management organization in line with the formal ERM recommendations around a corporate function that both supported risk management in the local national business entities and reported major exposures to top management. It was implemented in the wake of accusations, and actual incidents, of child labor abuse among sub-suppliers in Bangladesh. As time went by the risk management organization eventually became an integral part of the internal audit function, so the local business entities were controlled through regular audits to ensure compliance with the formal risk management processes. However, the implementation of formal risk management later monitored by internal audit did not prevent the company from allegedly being involved in $25 million of bribes paid by Vimpelcom (a partially owned firm) to obtain national telecom licenses.[14] The incident subsequently led to the resignation of the Chief Financial Officer and the General Counsel. The internal audit also uncovered suspicious transactions in Bangladesh and Thailand in 2015 and reported them to the local police (in one market). The internal audit committee later cleared the CEO but could obviously not prevent the incidents from happening.[15]

Again, the example illustrates how implementation of a formal ERM framework enforced by regular auditing processes seems to miss the ability to prevent unethical behaviors in high-level non-standardized business transactions.

And finally...

Volkswagen (VW)—The leading German automaker—used an internally developed risk management system for the group, mentioned in their annual reports, and they appear to have introduced a slightly more systematic ERM framework to structure risk management and internal controls from 2013 onwards. Volkswagen is a publicly listed company, but the ownership is still dominated by the founding families and the State of Lower Saxony who together hold decisive ownership interests in the company. During the period 2005–2008, Porsche, the much smaller high-end sports car manufacturer—that came out of the same family stock— attempted to take over Volkswagen. They almost succeeded in doing so, if it had not been for the unexpected event of the Lehman Brothers' collapse in September 2008. That event turned financial markets around and forced Porsche to unwind the financial positions that supported their takeover scheme. As events unfolded they were eventually themselves taken over by Volkswagen.[16]

In the wake of this debacle, Volkswagen's leadership pushed forward with an aggressive strategy, driven by the goal to become world leader in the industry, increasing sales by more than 10 million cars a year, and achieving a return on sales of at least 8%. These were very ambitious objectives and tough odds in difficult post-crisis market conditions. It is not hard to see that this ambition must have put the entire organization under a tremendous pressure to perform. Add to this the possible influence of a management style driven by relentless ambition with strict discipline and goal-orientation. Knowing full well that the formal argumentation for ERM is to support the realization of strategic objectives, it may be that the very risk management process—highlighted in the annual reports—became an implicit factor in enforcing the 'impossible' goals and as a consequence may have encouraged people within the organization to achieve these objectives by whatever means were required.

As is widely known, this led to the so-called 'Dieselgate' scandal, where Volkswagen (seemingly by pure accident) was caught manipulating the CO_2 emission data by installing a software device that was able to detect the testing conditions and thereby reduce the emissions during testing to pass the US regulatory standards. This scandal obviously touches upon some ethical dimensions and raises the simple question of how a big (otherwise well-reputed) company can let fraudulent things like this happen. It is not an easy problem to analyze and answer in a context 1) where the industry in general may be trying to avoid the harsh restrictions of tight pollution controls, 2) where German politicians to some extent try to forge the lead position of the national automobiles industry, and 3) where (many) US politicians seem to ignore the environmental concerns expressed in the regulatory emission standard. Nonetheless, the finger clearly points at VW with its top management ultimately being responsible for establishing an organizational context (or setting implicit expectations) that drove people to pursue these illicit activities to reach the performance outcomes that were expected of them.[17]

This widely publicized case illustrates the crucial role played by the emotional and ethical standing of top management in ways that no application of a formal risk management framework appears able to address or influence. While we recognize we are offering a speculative assessment, we see a fairly clear relationship between the 'irrational' emotional influences on the Volkswagen leadership after Porsche's takeover attempts and their ensuing quest to position Volkswagen as a world leading car manufacturer—come what may. It obviously also shows that even the most detailed, elaborate, and extensive ERM framework will never be able to capture the effects of these subtle leadership influences, nor detect and capture the type of risk factors that cause the 'Dieselgate' type of incidences.

Some thoughts on these stories

We do anticipate that some will see these illustrative stories as cherry-picked or even as cheap shots—serving more of a polemic than a descriptive purpose. We concede the point that one swallow does not a summer make. It is worth noting here, however, that we are not arguing that implementation of risk management according to the ERM practices invariably leads to bad outcomes. What we are trying to illustrate is that implementing ERM standards does not guarantee that the risk management practices actually follow espoused principles; neither does it seem well-suited to addressing the human dimension—particularly bad things instigated at the higher governance levels. So, we think the chosen examples make relevant and important points based on some factual and known corporate situations—and mind you, we could have chosen many other examples to show similar things.

So of course, the selective choice of case observations does not constitute a complete and unbiased data set on organizational ERM practices and failures. But in the wider context of our discussion, we stand by the view that these stories are indicative of a general insight. Hence, the number one challenge for risk leaders is to understand, anticipate, and address human behavior as a source of risk/uncertainty and concede that the ethical habits of the leadership are of critical importance. In saying this we are not intending to set an impossible standard. We will never be able to entirely prevent bad behavior and bad decision-making. And sometimes bad things just happen. But we should not act surprised to discover that it is, in fact, bad or improperly informed behavior (both conscious and unconscious) that underlies—time and again—most of the serious organizational failures.

Having spent much of our adult lives in academia, and specifically in business schools, we are mindful that our views may have—almost—a heretical bent. Business schools perform very important roles and—in recent years—have even made sincere efforts to think outside the realm of management theory and practice. Thus, courses on ethics, philosophy, critical thinking, and even religious thought have enjoyed a kind of ascendancy. These additions are to be roundly applauded, and the only thing we would add is that training for managers and leaders—including as it does matters of science, technology, systems, and processes—needs to become even more firmly infused with matters of the heart and soul. More Shakespeare and Montaigne and less (with apologies) 'Advanced Topics in Financial Management'—all elements in a proper balance.

GETTING BACK TO SOME DETAIL ON HUMAN BEHAVIOR AND PERCEPTION

The issues that arise in the space between espoused risk management and risk management in practice are explainable by recognizing that guidelines for risk management are advising people what to do but are not particularly oriented toward understanding how humans actually see the world and behave within that perceived environment. We intend to provide ballast to our argument in the following sections by briefly touching on perception, values, and behavior—obviously, as they pertain to uncertainty. We hope to tread lightly here as the matter of human perception, belief, and behavior requires a reasonably sturdy understanding of human psychology, anthropology, biology, genetics, and—well—a number of fields of study that examine how humans perceive and behave in the world. Our intention is not to cover these fields comprehensively but simply to introduce and illustrate key points.

Perception

Behavioral psychologists have revolutionized the way we think about economic agents and managerial decision-makers and, in fact, they have had similar impacts in a range of other fields. They have emphasized that there are different ways of defining *rational behavior* and that the classic utility-maximizing formulation that underlies not just classical economic theory but also a great deal of management thinking has significant limitations. In order to understand risk and uncertainty, we need to first understand how humans perceive these two aspects of the life we live. Daniel Kahneman's book, *Thinking, Fast and Slow*, is a notable but far from sole treatment this subject has received in recent years.[18]

For indicative purposes here, some general assertions that behavioral psychologists make are:

1. Essentially everything is uncertain, but it is impossible to live acknowledging that fact at all times in our daily lives, so we have developed ways in which we can act *as if* some things largely are certain.
2. These certainty-creating/uncertainty-reducing stratagems (sometimes called mental heuristics) work well enough most of the time, but they can be a source of further uncertainty inasmuch as we know they sometimes lead to problematic conclusions and actions.
3. Working with others in an open and inquisitive manner—being attentive and listening to others—can address some of the limitations that individuals bring to understanding our world, but not always.
4. One of the real challenges is that our 'fast' thinking is easy, and mainly produces useful outcomes that do not require much effort. 'Slow' thinking—let us call it critical thinking—really takes a great deal of effort. Further, it is nearly impossible to do it always and at all times. Additionally, the capacity to step outside ourselves and

think about our thinking is—let us admit—challenging. Even the ancient Greek philosophers recognized that knowing oneself was both essential but also difficult to achieve. So did Bertrand Russell, for that matter.

5. In one important sense, our human mental capacities have produced a paradox in that our minds and labors have built a world populated by many complexities that our brains have not fully evolved to comprehend—at least to comprehend without great difficulty. It is sometimes said that humans live in a highly complex world they have, themselves, built but must live in that world with Neolithic brains.

Heuristics, to return to that term, are rules of thumb intended to increase our ability to interpret a situation quickly, albeit not instantaneously.[19] Humans widely employ heuristics and indeed we might think of uncertainty-related heuristics as the 'quick risk assessment tool kit' we all possess. However, it will be important for us to recognize that heuristics have limitations. The heuristics relate to (fast unconscious) pattern-recognition capabilities that identify effective response effects, and when this happens, it frequently is adequate. This approach works quite well as long as the underlying events constitute relatively standard, representative, and repetitive phenomena, but is more problematic when confronting new unusual and untested situations.

But even heuristics linked to standard or repetitive events can become problematic. For example, the US Chemical Safety and Hazard Investigation Board found that the operators at the BP owned Texas City Refinery routinely ignored a number of warning signs. They knew the system was imperfect but nothing ever happened when they disregarded the alarms—until that day in March 2005 when a hydrocarbon vapor cloud ignited in a violent explosion that killed 15 workers and injured another 180 people. In another example the Rogers Commission investigating the Space Shuttle *Challenger* disaster in January 1986 also found a flawed decision-making culture—a generally accepted behavior, or heuristic, if you will. It was general knowledge that the O-rings that sealed the space shuttle's solid rocket booster had a design weakness, but it was ignored presumably because it was a recognized issue and it had never caused any previous incidents (before it eventually did of course, and then it was too late to respond).

Just to reinforce the point, let us just consider a couple of well-studied examples. The *anchoring* heuristic is a predisposition to make a judgment by starting from an initial value or 'anchor' and then making adjustments from that point. Human perceptions of other people or situations can—and do—change over time, but there is considerable research-based evidence to support the notion that people (only slowly) adjust their views in relation to their original position. Further, that initial impression or interpretation lingers and continues to influence the adjustments—even in instances when the initial estimate, let us say, is wildly off the mark. First impressions do matter, and they present stubborn resistance to alteration.

The *availability* heuristic is a predisposition to base judgments of probability on information or recollections that are readily available, while the related *representative* heuristic is a predisposition to base judgments of probability on things that are familiar. Humans are greatly influenced by events, people, situations that can be easily recalled from past observations and experience. Characteristics of these simple heuristics are: 1) recent events tend to be given more significance than long-ago events; 2) events that are not easily understandable are viewed as more unsettling than those that—while perhaps yielding distressing results—are due to understandable forces; and 3) near-by events are viewed as more threatening than far-away events.

It should be mentioned here that the modern media have an interesting impact in that it can produce a sense of immediate and imminent peril. For example, via television the 9/11 attacks occurred in our living rooms and were repeated over and over again. We could say that technology overrides the availability and representativeness heuristics, leading to rather interesting (although often irrational) effects. It has been theorized that global media is one reason humans feel less safe today than in previous time periods. Our mental risk assessment processing has been 'tricked' by the seeming proximity of tsunamis, earthquakes, volcanoes, terrorist attacks, and other events that are presented in the media as being both 'near-by,' 'frequent,' and 'horrific.' A good headline is a better way of selling (consciously or subconsciously) the news across competing media—and thus we have to add the media's motives and incentives to the list of influences on what we actually perceive.

Framing is another important heuristic. It refers to the idea that the context or frame of a particular situation can influence how one looks at that situation. For example, if a person is offered a 10% chance to win $10,000, this bet is likely to sound appealing. However, if additional information is provided indicating that losing the bet will require the gambler to have his hand amputated, well, that changes the context doesn't it? Our judgment of a risk can be greatly influenced by the inclusion or omission of relevant information and by the context in which that information is presented. A report on some bad news will likely be viewed differently if it is delivered on a stand-alone basis than if it is included with several reports containing good news (a ploy that pretty much everyone has used when bringing home a less-than-positive school report card).

OK, so this thing about heuristics is obviously very interesting 'academic stuff,' but you might venture to ask whether the heuristics really are that influential in the world of business. Hersh Shefrin, the Mario L. Belotti Professor of Finance at Santa Clara University, actually demonstrates that the global financial crisis of 2008 was significantly generated by these types of psychological pitfalls arguing that: "The root cause of the financial crisis that erupted in 2008 is psychological."[20] This was obviously enacted by the cumulative effect of irrational decisions made by many actors along the financial industry value-chain all the way from loan originators, bank intermediaries, financial analysts, rating agencies, and the eventual institutional investors.

Managers, executives, and boards were all, to differing degrees, affected by flawed assumptions about the continuity of historical house price developments and default rates. Behaviors came into alignment through such influences as benchmarking to common reference-points, group-think enhanced through mutual confirmation, and moral hazards caused by actors deemed 'too big to fail' that drove excessive risk-taking behaviors. This was further exacerbated by unethical behaviors that accepted weaker risk assessment criteria to obtain easy economic gains and grow the business volume as well as a poor incentive structure favoring short-term gains for long-term performance. Add to this the growing over-confidence among executive decision-makers that continued to generate handsome profits (due to their superior leadership competencies) but also among regulators that managed to indirectly enable the overconfident behavior. Yes, it all sounded good until it no longer did, and then the financial crisis was upon us.

It is all pretty clear that human emotions and sentiments were involved here and that a number of psychological biases were at play. Hence, Hersh Shefrin makes the sobering observation that "assuming that financial institutions will make intelligent, bias-free risk-reward decisions is a mistake." We can obviously extend this to all types of business organizations, and public institutions for that matter, where humans are involved. Again, to borrow from Hersh Shefrin: "Learning that decision makers have psychological biases is an important lesson … the lesson applies at all times, a point to keep in mind even as economic conditions improve." So, yes heuristics are important.

Several practical considerations arise from our quick look at heuristics. Everything is uncertain and thus while our quest to quantify uncertainty is worthwhile, and even admirable, our main concern should be around the unquantifiable phenomena that we encounter. Additionally, our cognitive abilities are, themselves, a source of risk and uncertainty—a first-order issue for risk managers/leaders. There are additional implications, but let's move on.

Beyond mental faculties, other factors are at play in how we perceive risk and uncertainty. There is genetic research indicating that some people have a propensity to seek risk, craving the endorphin rush, while others are innately risk averse. Cultures also play a role in influencing perception of risk. And, obviously, individual upbringing and personal experience can shape perceptions as well.

Perhaps a bit more should be said about culture. Social cultures play a large role, but individual organizations develop cultures and professions (engineers, lawyers) do as well. Indeed, it is likely that any one person might be subject to influence by various—and often competing—cultural factors. Social cultural influences can be among the harder to detect and address, largely because they often are the result of shared, unspoken, non-specific factors that shape the way we see and do things. For our purposes here, let us focus on a few central ideas that initially come from Mary Douglas[21] via John Adams in his seminal book *Risk*.[22]

Cultures do many things but they broadly influence perceptions of who is in and who is out of the group, which requires means of policing the boundaries, formal and informal rules for internal group behavior and relations, and expectations for relations with outside groups. The culture also shapes the group's relationship with its environment, which requires the group to understand the nature of that environment and the group's specific relationship to it. Some cultural expressions influence beliefs that emphasize hierarchy, while others do not. Some prize individuality, while others emphasize the integrity of the group. Some cultures reveal a sensibility that the environment is robust, tolerant, and immutable, where others see the environment as wildly unpredictable or precariously balanced on the edge of disaster. Beyond this, of course, cultures reveal philosophical and religious underpinnings that connect to values and beliefs. 'Origin myths,' for example, might be partly seen as providing answers to the questions, 'Who are we? Where did we come from?'

The point of this brief digression is just to note that there are many profound forces influencing how risk and uncertainty are perceived. They are all deemed to be worthy of attention as they influence how decisions are made in response to risk and uncertainty. This will be important to remember because, as John Adams notes (quoting Samuel Johnson): "it is hard to arrive at solutions when parties are arguing from different premises."

As an example, this can be observed in the debate over climate change. Since the unequivocal, iron-clad answer to the climate change question is only absolutely verified in the extreme long run, the debate is driven by perception and belief, under the shadow of highly persuasive but still not utterly conclusive data. Even when considering these realistic backdrops to differing opinions, the decisions and responsive actions taken as a consequence of these underlying beliefs are yet influenced by other psychological biases, i.e., can we always be sure that the chosen policies will actually achieve what they promise? Are these decisions sometimes more symbolic than real? The answer is probably yes, and this calls for a risk management approach that can help us engage in critical *thinking* for better decision-making.

This blunt assessment of the 'irrational' influence of uncertainty is a frustrating and worrying idea for many and could lead to the conclusion that risk management is simply a subjective exercise, i.e., it is situational, perceptual, and without objective foundation. This is not true, we believe. The climate is either changing in some permanent way or it is not. However, what is very much worth keeping in mind is the fact that none of us is likely to get *fully irrefutable* validation of our view within our lifetime.

Importantly, this seems to be a common element of many of the most important risks and uncertainties today. There is an objective dimension to these risks, but either the scope, scale, or timeframe is so wide or deep that we are left to debate the issues based on conjecture, theory, or limited objective data (or, let us be honest, prejudice and personal opinion). Thus, while it is certainly the case that research and analysis can improve our foothold on and understanding of the objective facts, we are mainly contesting our views of important challenges in a largely subjective sphere. If this is where the debate is waged, risk leaders need to understand this.

A curiosity worthy of mention

In his meditation on the role of luck in our lives, economist Robert H. Frank's book, *Success and Luck: Good Fortune and the Myth of Meritocracy*, offers a compelling look at the phenomenon of luck and—critically here—how humans perceive luck. We might, for our purposes, slightly stretch the concept of luck to include 'fortune and probability,' as those words certainly possess at least an affiliate status.[23]

Through the lens of his own personal experiences (adoption, and a near-death health episode) Frank develops a thesis around our perception of luck and its impact on our lives. Although it simplifies his theme a bit, we might say that humans value the role of luck differently and that we might imagine a spectrum of views ranging from the belief that luck plays no role in our life story, to one where luck is seen as the predominant influence. Frank believes luck tends—on balance—to be the more undervalued of life's possible influences.

There are at least three relevant thoughts that derive from Frank's deliberations:

1. If luck is undervalued, does that mean our ability to recognize and value the impact of happenstance, probability, fortune, or unlucky hops influences our ability to judge our uncertain world? In practical terms is there then an inherent barrier to delivering and accepting the risk management message?
2. It seems that individuals who rise to leadership levels in organizations (and societies) may partially be the products of an inherent selection process that rewards individuals who view success as the result of their own personal attributes and hard work—rather than good fortune. If so, how does this influence the top decision-maker's reception of the risk management message?
3. The implication of Frank's thesis is that we need to recognize the role of luck in our lives, but this gives rise to a question: 'How much recognition do we need to give luck?' After all, if a CEO were to believe her present success was only due to luck, how persuasive and dynamic a leader would she be? Would anyone follow for long a person who believes fortune is the primary determinant of outcomes? Confidence in oneself seems to matter too.

Here it is probably sufficient to be alert to the idea that this is a dynamic in play within the C-Suite and boardrooms. Since critical thinking is assumed to support effective communication and persuasion, it seems that understanding distinctive perspectives shared by the specific target audience would require some special care.

Richard Wiseman in his book, *The Luck Factor*, demonstrates how luck is associated with four simple principles that guide the way we live and act.[24] So, according to his findings lucky individuals—lucky in the sense that they achieve success in different dimensions of their lives—display a number of common characteristics:

1. They notice and act upon observed opportunities by maintaining a strong network of contacts, having a relaxed attitude to life and an open attitude to new experiences.
2. They stay alert to their intuitive lucky hunches and listen to their gut feelings, boosting their intuition, being open to emerging opportunities.

3. They believe the future will help them fulfill their dreams expecting good fortune, achieving success, and expecting lucky relationships in interactions with other people.
4. They turn bad luck into good fortune by seeing the positive side of bad luck, keeping a positive outlook, taking steps to prevent deterioration.

This is interesting in the sense that human beliefs and attitudes seem to be essential factors that drive individual human success—or luck—and that organizations then may be able to create organizational climates or settings that facilitate these personal sentiments and attitudes possibly as structural and cultural artifacts. If this is so, then the leadership role of creating the 'right' organizational culture becomes an essential aspect of effective risk management. Richard Wiseman rightly points to the fact that many important developments in our personal lives and major scientific discoveries happen by accident—or luck—as is the case with many path-breaking inventions that have formed entire commercial enterprises. So, the ability to capture, in some sense, the 'individual luck' of organizational members may be an important aspect of risk management in environments that need successful responses to uncertain and unpredictable developments.

It is still essential that the values imbedded in an organizational culture aspire to carry out good deeds—for a broader set of stakeholders—as opposed to fostering unethical, narrow, and self-interested behaviors. This requires the leaders to exemplify those values in practice—through real actions—setting an example and 'walking the talk' as we say.[25] If the executive actions and decisions fail to reflect the espoused values, the members of the organization will lose faith and render the pronounced aims as being false and unworthy of support, which is detrimental to good performance.

Values

Business ethicist, Ken Goodpaster, formulates a framework for envisioning risk and uncertainty in the context of values and beliefs.[26] His concept of *teleopathy* poses the idea that ethical 'risks' arise from disconnections between Goals, Means, and Values. Notably here, he acknowledges the centrality of goals or objectives in organizational settings but challenges us to recognize that how we go about pursuing those goals matters, and how our values influence and govern our decisions and actions also matters. In this three-cornered relationship we not only see the elements of what we identify as ethical risks, but—frankly—we witness the so-called garden plot for most major organizational crises, scandals, and disasters.

Values-and-means risks seem characterized by what lengths we will go to to accomplish our goals. Not obviously stated, but implicit in the concept of teleopathy, is the relationship between organizational (or situation-specific) values and broader societal values (or 'Values'). After all, we might have tightly woven goals, values, and means all serving reprehensible ends. So, ultimately, a fourth area of imbalance might arise between values and Values: Do the organizational values reflect accepted societal values?

Volkswagen's Dieselgate affair might be a good case in point. Setting very ambitious goals for the organization and its global competitive position can be a strong motivation for employees but only if the moral compass that directs the organizational aspirations coincide with the aims of society, and not against them, or even at the expense of society.

From a management perspective, then, recent high-profile events have produced a sharp portrait of the practical consequences of unethical and irresponsible conduct—which are often evidence of the gulf between espoused values and values in action. Indeed, these consequences have led to impacts with which risk managers are quite familiar: loss of reputation, legal penalties, dislocation of workers, credit rating downgrades, demands for greater oversight and new rules. Set in these terms, ethical considerations are very much like conventional risks where human behavior and choice can lead to positive or negative outcomes. The question does arise, however, what/whose values?

Many answers are possible, but just to give this discussion some substance, we briefly consider the Caux Round Table (CRT). It is an international network of business leaders working to promote moral capitalism.[27] Though CRT is most focused on finding globally consistent business values and principles, we think something might be gained here by considering CRT thinking with respect to the pursuit of universal principles and values in relation to risk and uncertainty.

The CRT Principles are rooted in two basic ethical ideals: *kyosei* and *human dignity*. According to CRT:

> [t]he Japanese concept of *kyosei* means living and working together for the common good, enabling cooperation and mutual prosperity to coexist with healthy and fair competition. *Human dignity* refers to the sacredness or value of each person as an end, not simply as a means to the fulfillment of others' purposes or even majority prescription.

The resulting CRT framework rests on the following eight principles:

1. The responsibilities of businesses: beyond shareholders toward stakeholders.
2. The economic and social impact of business: toward innovation, justice and world.
3. Community.
4. Business behavior: beyond the letter of the law toward a spirit of trust.
5. Respect for rules.
6. Support for multilateral trade.
7. Respect for the environment.
8. Avoidance of illicit operations.

Each of these aspirational principles might be said to represent 'Global Values' in the sense that the Caux Round Table seeks to establish its principles as a value-system for global corporate culture. We believe these values can be used to consider issues that cover a potentially comprehensive range of ethical risks (and by inference, governance risks). It should be noted that the Caux Round Table has lost some momentum from its early years, and some controversies have arisen regarding its methodologies, but we think the general ideas espoused stand as an indicator of how the dynamic between values and Values might look in distinctly global settings.

Some further thoughts on ethical risks

Developing, implementing, and maintaining ethical business practices is not easy, and—indeed—we could say that the effort to do so could be a source of risk and uncertainty itself.[28] One clear framing issue is the tendency to look at this effort in legalistic terms. Does our work comply with Sarbanes-Oxley, Dodd-Frank, Federal Sentencing Guidelines, UN Global Compact, the Consumer Charter for Global Business, and so on? Legal behavior is important, but 'we broke no laws' will always ring hollow as a defense. Ethicists have argued that amoral behaviors ultimately cannot be adequately policed through rules and regulations but have to rely on *virtue*; that is, via an organizational culture that aspires to virtuous behavior.

We instinctively know, and recent research confirms, that a discrepancy between espoused values and those that are actually practiced in the organization can lead to bad outcomes.[29] We have already presented a few cases to illustrate the point. For example, Vestas stated that it put an emphasis on good risk management, but the process was swept aside when push came to shove. Nokia claimed that everyone in the organization was responsible for identifying risks, yet top management was deaf to the warnings from the engineers that sensed what was going on. Volkswagen tried to appear to be a green company, but in reality forgot and/or pushed people to commit unethical acts to reach the overambitious goals set by the leadership.

Another important point to remember here is that the poor behavior of the leadership will trickle down through the organization where employees and middle managers reason that if top management can act this way, then so can I, or I owe them no allegiance when they show this kind of morality, and I will defy them.[30]

BP is an interesting example to illustrate the role of corporate values and ethical risks. The board of BP installed Tony Heyworth as new CEO in 2007 after the Texas City Refinery explosion that killed numerous workers and cost the company compensation payments in excess of US$1 billion. He tried to institute reforms to avoid similar incidents and establishing a 'Code of Conduct' to guide the actions of people working in the company. What did the code emphasize? It covered the key areas of business operations, the first one being: Health, safety, security and the environment to protect the natural environment; safety of communities where the company operates, and the health, safety and security of the people working there.

For the sake of simplicity, let us focus on the first one—health, safety, security and the environment, which is pretty clear and unambiguous. Yet, it did not prevent another major and comparable incident from occurring. In April 2010 the BP commissioned oil rig, *Deepwater Horizon*, operating in the Mexican Gulf exploded killing 11 men under its stewardship and creating the largest environmental disaster in US history. As one consequence, Tony Heyworth's three-year reign as CEO was terminated, but what is intriguing—to put it mildly—is the fact that the entire organization from the board to the lead engineers in charge of the field operations acted in stark contrast to the very first point of the Code of Conduct—probably without even thinking about it.[31] They were so used to working under the strain of extreme project deadlines and time pressures, competing globally to get oil out of the ground to advance the company in a tough business environment, and a relentless drive to report positive news and quarterly earnings to the shareholders.

This illustrates the vivid contrast we see many times between what is being said and publicly pronounced to look good, and what is really going on within the organization. It also shows that the heuristics and engrained behaviors often are embedded in the organizational culture and core values in very subtle, even invisible, ways that might only be traced in retrospective analyses. In short, the true values are not always those you see espoused in a glossy Annual Report or CSR Report. They are found in the actual behaviors and enacted decisions that often are only observed after the fact.

Behavior

How do people then behave as a result of their perceptions, culture, and values? Again, the primary conclusion here is that it rarely aligns with utility-maximization. Self-preservation might be a better summarizing assessment, but even then, not always. A well-known post-event analysis of the 1987 King's Cross London Underground station fire found that when encountering the fire, the behavior of both staff and passengers did not track with the expectations one might assume would be seen.[32]

Probably the essential point to address here is that humans do not react in entirely predictable ways, or to be slightly more precise, they do tend to react in predictable ways—just not the ways we think they would tend to react as so-called rational beings. It is for this reason that many assumptions about risk management applications need to be qualified or at least carefully considered. We have already identified moral hazard as a phenomenon that defines how the introduction of a risk management measure might change people's behavior (and not always in positive ways). But even absent some risk management intervention, we need to understand risks and uncertainties, not just in terms of their objective properties but also in terms of how people react to them.

Understanding human behavior under conditions of uncertainty could and can lead to risk management decisions that seem counter-intuitive. For example, it might be that the best solution in some high-risk situations is to do nothing. An extremely treacherous mountain road may not benefit from the installation of guard rails, as those guard rails may promote more unsafe driving that leads to more accidents. The logic in that simple illustration is that it is better for those exposed to danger to have a full and accurate appreciation of that danger rather than giving individuals a false sense of security and safety.

Hersh Shefrin concludes that: "Risk management involves risks associated with human vulnerabilities just as much as risk is associated with physical phenomena and market conditions."

We obviously concur with that. He further argues that "Psychological pitfalls associated with emotions, framing effects, heuristics, and biases create major risks, and these are risks to be managed."[33] This insight obtained from years of studies in behavioral corporate finance and financial market behaviors is aligned with our thinking about some of the overlooked factors in the risk management field. We can observe how cognitive biases among key decision-makers and the processing of risk information among different organizational constituents can mold and distort the basis for decisions particularly in uncertain and unpredictable contexts. This is a key challenge for modern risk management.

Part of the answer might be gathered from Aswath Damodaran's first principle of risk management:

> Our biggest risks will come from places that we least expect them to come from and in forms that we did not anticipate that they would take. The essence of good risk management is to be able to roll with the punches when confronted with the unexpected.[34]

This seems to imply a larger degree of flexibility than appears to be afforded in existing control-based risk management frameworks and enabling both distributed risk-taking in a facilitating organization structure—guided by proper corporate values—and interactive processing of updated risk information.

In any event, we believe that understanding perception, values, and ethical behaviors constitutes the so-called wheel-house for effectively addressing risk and uncertainty, and it suggests that risk managers/leaders need to have an appropriate level of understanding of these challenges.

EVEN MORE TO THINK ABOUT ...

Many of the serious effects of heuristics, cognitive biases, and other psychological pitfalls are linked to the ethical conduct of top management and the board. But how can we consider the importance of ethical behavior, values, and organizational culture, their impact on performance outcomes, and the risk management approaches needed to achieve positive outcomes?

To this end we again draw on the work by Goodpaster (this time with colleagues) where their scholarship has developed a model of ethical business cultures. The five model characteristics of an ethical business culture are values-driven, leadership effectiveness, stakeholder balance, process integrity, and long-term perspective:

1. **Values-driven.** Values are defined by character and are above compromise with any expediency or gain. Values form the

organizational culture, organizational culture determines or reflects how leaders behave, how stakeholders are treated, how internal processes function, and the degree to which the organization's perspective is long term. Ethical cultures display two distinct languages or syntaxes. One takes its cue from *espoused values*; the other is a language of *values-in-action*. Tensions between stated and practiced values can have a significant impact on operational effectiveness. In other words, success within the organization rests upon a harmonious interaction between the stated values that characterize desired behavior within the organization and the practiced values that moderate and reinforce the actual behavior within an organization's core business functions and processes.

2. **Leadership effectiveness.** Leadership, most notably senior management, must embody the organization's values in its own behavior and must articulate those values in a way that is compelling for employees and all other stakeholders.

3. **Stakeholder balance.** Refers to the central premise of stakeholder theory, which is that organizations and their managers have fiduciary and other responsibilities to various stakeholder groups who have a vested interest in the success of their organizations. Stakeholder balance suggests that tensions can and do exist between multiple stakeholders, and recognition of this can lead to a forum for discussion and consideration of various stakeholder concerns.

4. **Process integrity.** Describes the institutionalization of the company's values throughout its business activities and operations across various units and entities including key functions like recruiting, hiring, firing, evaluating, compensating, promoting, communicating, and managing.

5. **Long-term perspective.** The long-term perspective involves a balance between short-term actions and long-term aims. It implies doing what is right—not what is easy. Failing to do things right in the short term can create (a lot of) harm in the long term.

This model can provide a basis for analyzing and assessing the ethical risk status of an organization—and not least, compare the espoused values to the values deployed into practice along these five elemental dimensions.

In the ensuing, and final, chapter, we will set out our views of risk management with some suggested ways of converting our thoughts into practical use.

NOTES

1   Russell, Bertrand (1933). The triumph of stupidity, in *Mortals and Others: Bertrand Russell's Essays, 1931–1935*. Routledge: London.
2   Bargeron, L., Lehn, K. and Zutter, C. (2010). Sarbanes-Oxley and corporate risk-taking. *Journal of Accounting and Economics* 49(1–2): 34–52.
3   *The Risk Minds 2009 Risk Managers' Survey: The Cause and Implications of the 2008 Banking Crisis*. Moore, Carter & Associates/Cranfield School of Management 2010.
4   Aebi, V., Sabato, G. and Schmid, M. (2012). Risk management, corporate governance, and bank performance in the financial crisis. *Journal of Banking & Finance*, 36: 3213–3226. Beltratti, A. and Stulz, R.M. (2009). *Why did some banks perform better during the credit crisis? A cross-country study of the impact of governance and regulation (No. w15180)*. National Bureau of Economic Research.
5   See, for example, Smith, Adam (2009). *The Theory of Moral Sentiments*. Penguin Books: New York (first pulished in 1759).
6   Andersen, T.J. (2010). Lehman Brothers (B), Case Centre #310-265-1.
7   See, for example, McDonald, L. (2009). *A Collosal Failure of Common Sense: The Incredible Inside Story of the Collapse of Lehman Brothers*. Ebury Press: London.
8   Mitroff, A. and Silvers, I. (2010). *Dirty Rotten Strategies: How We Trick Ourselves and Others Into Solving the Wrong Problems Precisely*. Stanford Business Books: Stanford, CA.
9   Finkelstein, Sydney (2003). *Why Smart Executives Fail*. Penguin Books: New York.
10 See, for example, Prahalad, C.K. (2004). *Fortune at the Bottom of the Pyramid: Eradicating Poverty Through Profits*. Prentice Hall: Upper Saddle River, NJ.
11 Andersen, T.J. (2018). *Case: Nokia—The Rise and Fall of an Icon*. Copenhagen Business School.
12 Anthony, Scott D. (2016). Kodak's downfall wasn't about technology. *Harvard Business Review July* 15, 2016.
13 Telia Sonera Annual Report 2007.
14 AFP (news@thelocal.no). Norway's Telenor in corruption scandal, November 15, 2014. www.thelocal.no/20141115/norways-telenor-in-bribe-scandal.
15 Gyana Ranjan Swan (2016). Telenor Accepts Mass Corruption At Its Asia Biz, Clears CEO Brekke. *Tele Analysis*, December 13. www.teleanalysis.com/news/telenor-accepts-mass-corruption-asia-operation-clears-ceo-brekke-23951
16 Andersen, T.J. (2010). *Case: Porsche (D)*. Copenhagen Business School.
17 Various sources, e.g., Bovens, L. (2016). The Ethics of Dieselgate. *Midwest Studies in Philosophy, XL* and Siano, A., Vollero, A., Conte, F. and Amabile, S. (2017). More than words: Expanding the taxonomy of greenwashing after the Volkswagen scandal. *Journal of Business Research*.
18 Kahneman, D. (2011). *Thinking, Fast and Slow*. Penguin Books: London.
19 One of the earlier works that addresses behavior under conditions of uncertainty is Tversky, A. and Kahneman, D. (1992). Advances in prospect theory: Cumulative representation of uncertainty. *Journal of Risk and Uncertainty*, 5(4): 297–323.
20 Shefrin, Hersh (2016). How psychological pitfalls generated the global financial crisis, in Andersen, T.J. (ed.), *The Routledge Companion to Strategic Risk Management*, pp. 269–295.
21 Dame Mary Douglas, DBE FBA was a British anthropologist who is known for her writings on and insights about human culture and symbolism.

22 Adams, John. (1995). *Risk*. Routledge: London.

23 Frank, Robert H. (2016). *Success and Luck: Good Fortune and the Myth of Meritocracy*. Princeton University Press: Princeton, NJ.

24 Wiseman, Richard (2003). *The Luck Factor*. Arrow Books: London.

25 Andersen, T.J. (2017). Corporate responsible behavior in multinational enterprise. *International Journal of Organizational Analysis*, 25(3): 1–21.

26 Kenneth E. Goodpaster. (2007). *Conscience and Corporate Culture*. Blackwell: Malden, MA.

27 The Caux Round Table for Moral Capitalism, Website. www.cauxroundtable. org

28 This insight emerges, at least indirectly, in considerable business ethics research, including: Ardichvili, A., Mitchell, J. and Jondle, D. (2009) Characteristics of ethical business cultures. *Journal of Business Ethics*, 85: 445–451; and Feldman, S. (2007). Moral business cultures: The keys to creating and maintaining them. *Organizational Dynamics*, 36: 156–170.

29 Minbaeva, D., Rabbiosi, L. and Stahl, G.K. (2018). Not walking the talk? How host country cultural orientations may buffer the damage of corporate values' misalignment in multinational corporations. *Journal of World Business*, 53(6): 880–895.

30 A good discussion on the influence of leaders on the organization is found in Bass, B.M. and Steidlmeier, P. (1999). Ethics, character, and authentic transformational leadership behavior. *Leadership Quarterly*, 10: 181–218.

31 Andersen, T.J. and Andersen, C.B. (2014). *Case: British Petroleum—From Texas City to the Gulf of Mexico and Beyond*.Copenhagen Business School.

32 A thorough-going analysis of this event is found in Desmond Fennell's *Investigation into the King's Cross Underground Fire*, produced for the UK Department of Transport in 1988.

33 Shefrin, Hersh (2016). *Behavioral Risk Management: Managing the Psychology the Drives Decisions and Influences Operational Risk*. Palgrave Macmillan: London, p. 335.

34 Damodaran, Aswath (2008). *Strategic Risk Taking: A Framework for Risk Management*. Wharton School Publishing: Upper Saddle River, NJ.

5 What, then, is risk management?

Anyone in public life who has strong convictions about the rights and wrongs of public morality ... has a very great advantage in times of strain, since his instincts on what to do are clear and immediate. What worries me are the conclusions that ... an individual [lacking such a framework of moral conviction] may reach when he is tired, angry, frustrated, or emotionally affected.

Chester Bowles[1]

The preceding quotation is drawn from one of the more powerful books ever written about the Vietnam War—David Halberstam's *The Best and the Brightest*. In one sense, citing his book risks being something of a paradox as one could say that the central theme is 'smart people making bad decisions.' In our defense, we never make the claim that smart people are free from the many psychological traps that befall humans— far from it, as Halberstam painfully reveals. Indeed, we believe the more proper way to interpret the Bowles' quote is to say, 'Look, critical thinking is really hard. Even very smart people can make horrendous decisions. Effective risk management/leadership is not easy to implement and maintain.' Beyond that, note that Bowles zeros in on a point we have already made about the centrality of values in making decisions under conditions of uncertainty.

What really would be paradoxical would be the two of us not subjecting ourselves to the same standard of critical thinking. What if we are wrong? Indeed, we could say that the willingness to be challenged, to be skeptical of our own views, is the only stance possible for risk managers/leaders. It is sometimes said that the essence of risk management is found in the question, 'How might I/we be wrong?' That is, we have worked hard to understand an issue, to measure it, to consider its impacts, to develop appropriate responses—but—what if we have gotten it wrong? Wrong decision-makers, wrong assumptions, unawareness of critical factors, wrong decision processes, wrong framing of issues, and on and on. We will try to hold ourselves to this standard in Chapter 5.

We are going to depart from our approach in Chapters 2, 3, and 4 where we end with an example or small case study. We start this chapter with our case and use it as a somewhat uplifting story about effective risk management/leadership, and then set out several ideas that arise from the case, but which also extend several key discussion points from this book.

A HOPEFUL STORY

The South Dakota State Legislature created the South Dakota Science and Technology Authority (SDSTA) in 2004 to foster scientific and technological investigations, experimentation, and development in South Dakota. A six-member board of directors appointed by the governor directs the SDSTA.

The precipitating event in this story was the closure of the Homestake Gold Mine, by some measures the largest goldmine ever to operate in the Western Hemisphere, and certainly one of the largest employers in South Dakota. Through an intense effort to consider economic development responses, the state of South Dakota decided to focus on basic scientific research as a possible avenue of recovery and engaged Homestake in discussion about somehow obtaining use of the mine. As a result, in 2006 the SDSTA Board of Directors accepted Barrack Mining Company's (which owned Homestake) donation of the underground mine and 186 surface acres.

A document called the Property Donation Agreement (PDA) dictated the terms of that gift. Also in 2006, the SDSTA accepted a $70 million gift from South Dakota philanthropist T. Denny Sanford, who stipulated that $20 million of the donation be used for a Sanford Science Education Center. Both donations were contingent upon the National Science Foundation's (NSF's) selection of Homestake as the preferred site for a national Deep Underground Science and Engineering Laboratory (DUSEL). As part of that preliminary agreement SDSTA's first task was to reopen the former Homestake gold mine to the 4,850-foot depth-level for scientific research (the mine reaches a depth of nearly 8,000 feet).

The NSF made that selection on July 10, 2007, which triggered the SDSTA's reopening of Homestake. In December 2010, the NSF decided to halt continued funding of designs for DUSEL; however, within months the Department of Energy (DOE) took over sponsorship of the project. The DOE's approach to underground science at Homestake differed significantly from the DUSEL plan, but it did (and does) include support for current experiments and continued study of the feasibility of longer-term research. DOE began funding daily operations at the Lab in fiscal year 2012 through an agreement between the SDSTA and Lawrence Berkeley National Laboratory (LBNL), which then oversaw the project for the DOE. It was at this time, and partly due to the changes in funding source that DUSEL became SURF—the Sanford Underground Research Facility.

The SDSTA completed construction of laboratories on the 4,850-foot level in May 2012. The Davis Campus—named for the late Ray Davis, who pioneered neutrino research at Homestake—became home to two experiments: the Large Underground Xenon (LUX) dark matter detector and the Majorana Demonstrator neutrinoless double-beta decay experiment. Those experiments began taking data in 2013 and 2014. Meanwhile, the SDSTA expanded its project portfolio, notably initiating work with the Fermi National Accelerator Laboratory, the DOE, and the NSF on the development of additional experiments. Additionally, the SDSTA also built out the Sanford Center for Science Education and began offering pilot education programs for students of all ages. By 2019, the Sanford Laboratory continued to add projects and now has an extended multi-decade plan for a wide variety of new projects.

A quick look at the science

Researchers at SURF go deep underground to try to answer some of the most challenging physics questions about the universe. What is the origin of matter? What is dark matter and how do we know it exists? What are the properties of neutrinos? Sanford Lab is located at a historically significant landmark for basic physics research. As noted previously, nuclear chemist Ray Davis first recognized the potential for deep science in the mid-1960s when he built his solar neutrino experiment at Homestake. In 2002, his ground-breaking research earned him the Nobel Prize in Physics.

Why do scientists go so deep underground to study particles that come from the universe? On the surface, millions of cosmic rays pass through it every few months. But nearly a mile underground, it's a million times quieter. The rock acts as a natural shield, blocking most of the radiation that can interfere with sensitive physics experiments, and it turns out a mine's geologic environment is particularly suited to large physics experiments for another reason—the hard rock is perfect for excavating the large caverns needed for big experiments.

As noted, SURF now hosts world-leading research that can only be done in an underground environment. SURF works with many institutions and organizations around the globe including the DOE, National Science Foundation (NSF), NASA, Lawrence Berkeley National Laboratory (LBNL), and Fermi National Accelerator Laboratory (Fermilab). Sanford Lab also hosts experiments in other disciplines—including biology, geology, and engineering. Experiments include the search for life underground, gravitational waves, and seismic activity. Additionally, the Black Hills State University Underground Campus creates opportunities for students from universities across South Dakota and the world to develop research projects in a variety of disciplines.

The SURF risk management story

In many senses, the Sanford Laboratory is a risk management success story and—in fact—illustrates one of the observations made earlier about the long run. A vision of the long-run objectives is critical, but a focus on 'getting started' proved to be the key ingredient. In an interesting spin on conventional risk management thinking, the getting started phase involved extreme and conscious risk-taking. The Board of Directors undertook a process of determining the risks and concluded that while they had a high level of risk aversion, they would have to take aggressive risks to reopen the former goldmine, and then just be prepared to address risks and uncertainties as they encountered them (a resilience posture, though they were far from resilient in terms of the capacity to bear risk).

That approach, it is argued by SDSTA leadership, was aimed, first and foremost, at confidence-building; building confidence in themselves and the managerial team and then engendering the confidence or reputation among funders, taxpayers, and scientists. Another way to think about this is to say that the leadership team had no appetite for risk and uncertainty, but realized it had to accept a high tolerance of risk and uncertainty to improve confidence, generate trust, and build a good reputation around its ability to deliver a long-run outcome.

It should be noted that sheer luck has played a role—especially pertaining to NSF's sudden decision to stop funding the facility. But even here, we might note that the leadership team was highly sensitized to the overwhelming risk/uncertainty of the project and evolved a stance toward management that one might describe as risk aware, alert with a keen concern about the unknown. To repeat, this was a far from resilient organization, but its mindset was oriented toward resilience—and it was seeming to enjoy great success in 2019.[2] However, as one SDSTA leader humorously mentioned, "terror, panic, and a constant gnawing fear of failure served as important motivators as well."

We think this story pretty much tells it all. Risk management did not eradicate all problems. SDSTA enjoyed some successes but encountered failures too. There was not a lot of glamour present, nor high visibility nationally and internationally. Nevertheless, by the standards of the day, this was an incredibly high-risk situation that resulted in a broadly positive result—a result that is still unfolding today. Analytically, but not experientially (we are not sure anyone was overly conscious of the motives behind many decisions made), we think this story underscores a number of elements of our view of risk management and opens the door to a short discussion of each of those elements.

SOME INITIAL INSIGHTS ARISING FROM SDSTA/SURF (AND OUR BOOK)

The SDSTA/SURF story provides some scene-setting here by at least suggesting a set of key points from the book. We make slight alterations to the general thrust of the story to emphasize them:

1. What role do values play in risk management, and how do we integrate them into risk management?
2. Thinking about thinking.
3. Assessing risk, uncertainty, and the unknown.
4. Developing a mental map for understanding how organizations become exposed to risk, uncertainty, and the unknown.

In looking at these four issues, we hope to produce a set of suggestions that take our analysis beyond description and criticism, and offer some reasonably practical ideas about implementing risk management/ leadership in alignment with our general views.

The centrality of values

We hope we have planted—and even rooted—the idea that values guide risk managers/leaders in determining the proper course of action and should serve a critical influencing role in the decision-making processes. Though some decisions—even in the face of uncertainty—require detailed and sophisticated analysis, the very initial decision is to determine whether the possible courses of action align with the organization's espoused values. But, can we be a bit more explicit about the answer to the question, 'What values?' Can we always be sure that the espoused values expressed officially by the organization are valid and legitimate?

To this end we offer some guidance from the Catholic Identity Matrix (CIM) developed by the Veritas Institute at the University of St. Thomas. It is a good—but rare—example of a methodology developed to evaluate ethical standards and performance in an organization based on a self-assessment and improvement process (SAIP). Note here, that we are mindful that the majority of the world is not Catholic—neither are we, for that matter—but the foundation of the thinking here is broadly applicable as a frame of reference.

According to SAIP, organizations—that is, the people acting within them seeing an organization as a collection of moral agents—should adhere to the following five (or six—one may not be relevant in all situations) *ethical principles*, and do this consistently over time to maintain a moral corporate conscience:

1. Show solidarity with those who live in poverty.
2. Care for the whole—consider broader stakeholder concerns.
3. Respect human life and dignity.
4. Participate in the community and work for mutual respect.
5. Show stewardship—leadership supported care for moral behavior.
6. Act in communion with the church (relevant particularly to church-based health care providers).

The CIM provides an assessment of six *supportive tasks* the organization must be able to perform to address each of these ethical principles:

- Plan—reflect the ethical principles in mission and strategy deliberations.
- Align—support the principles in consistent performance and reward systems.
- Process—adopt the principles in the internal work processes and procedures.
- Train—provide people with the competencies needed to enact the principles.
- Measure—develop management information for process effectiveness.
- Impact—establish metrics to monitor the desired outcomes.

This provides the basis for a matrix to assess the extent to which an organization applies the (six) supportive tasks towards the accomplishment of the (five/six listed) ethical principles. While this represents a potential tool kit that may be seen as another box-ticking exercise, it does represent a way to deal more explicitly with the extremely important aspects of ethics and values in organizations and not least as a way to assess whether the espoused values correspond to values in action.[3]

The ideas set forward in the SAIP, we think, correspond quite closely to our line of thinking. They basically propose that in the absence of quantitative information on risk/uncertainty the decision rule is based on articulated and (more specifically) practiced values. Indeed, values should still inform decisions even when valid quantitative data are abundantly available for analysis. Recall our own risk management distinction between espoused values and values in action, and our belief that many—if not most—of the cited crises, disasters, and other key events fundamentally have values-related causes. In the SDSTA/SURF example, the highly political/social/economic dimension of the project put values front and center. This, after all, was a story about an economic disaster to a region of the country and the need for a very small state to find a way to create jobs, economic activity, and renewed energy in the development of that region. While it does not always happen in government and public policy, here was a situation where the centrality of values could not be easily ignored.

Thinking about thinking

In the SDSTA side of the story, it is worth noting that the technical detail of a basic research laboratory (alongside the technicalities of managing an extremely large mining facility), was of such a high level of sophistication that there was no way to build an advisory board of scholars and mine engineers with sufficient knowledge to be able to make early decisions. Additionally, there was a huge political and economic development dimension to the project, which demanded further expertise in those areas. Owing to this particularly challenging fact, the early days presented a patently overwhelming array of highly technical demands. The Board was keenly aware of the limits of its collective knowledge and was skeptical that it could make decisions without being very careful and seeking outside advice. Partly because of that very evident situation, a version of the following was employed to help the Board get its footing, especially with respect to risk and uncertainty.

In their 1986 book *Thinking in Time*, authors Richard Neustadt and Ernest May present a series of essays on the uses of history and historical research methodologies in modern management (particularly public management).[4] An underlying argument in this book is that most challenges faced by managers are similar in construct to those encountered by historians (i.e., data are limited and/or contradictory, information exists in many non-comparable forms, perspectives or points of view matter, the historian's perspective and own psychological makeup are ingredients in the story, and context is important to understand). The authors make several other critical observations, especially about stories as a framing device. To paraphrase it somewhat differently, but in line with our prior reasoning, Neustadt and May see the world as mainly uncertain—not risky.

It is important to note here that their book does not present a unified Neustadt-May method *per se*. Rather, they examine how the study of the historian's method can deal with and interpret uncertain contexts. So, we have chosen selected discussion points from their book that build out an organized analytical/decision approach. It is only for the reason of absolutely clear attribution that we use the label *Neustadt-May method* to summarize a process involving three sequential stages:

1. Development of the narrative.
2. Structuring the current context.
3. Framing the decision.

Development of the narrative. The critical first step is the development of a history of the very situation encountered by the manager, management, or decision-maker(s) and seeks to answer the central question: 'How did we get here?'

The creation of a narrative has two levels of logic. First, cause-and-effect relationships are important to understand when the end result is a practical risk management application. But second, and equally importantly, humans tend to better understand information revealed in a story format. Significant research in the areas of risk communication and the psychology of learning show that humans comprehend and process information that is represented in a narrative structure—perhaps not a surprising finding when one considers how complex legends and myths existed only in an oral form for hundreds of years.

The process of narrative development involves several steps and several questions. The first step is to decide where the narrative must begin. This is not always easy and, of course, it invariably must be somewhat arbitrary. One could seek to adopt a metaphysical point of view and start every narrative with Genesis, but practicality dictates some level of reasonableness here. However, the key to establishing a narrative format is to arrive at some plausible and defensible starting point.

The second step is to establish the parameters or boundaries of the narrative. Again, this element of narrative formation has a degree of arbitrariness, but it nevertheless is necessary to set narrative boundaries.

The third step is to clarify and establish the sequence and timing of key events. This is done by first setting the key 'plot points' (i.e., the driving or catalytic elements in the story). Plot points consist of one or more elements, of which there are four generic types: people, things, events, and situations. The final part of the third step is to connect the plot points along a narrative line.

The final step of narrative development is narrative assessment. Neustadt and May argue for a journalistic approach to narrative assessment, meaning that the assembled narrative is subjected to a 'who, where, what, why, and when' analysis as well as a self-critical exploration of the assessment (are we sure? what is the degree of confidence we have in this assessment? why might we be wrong?).

The result of this first stage is a provisional but reasonably solid story that can be accepted as the explanation for why the current circumstances exist as they do, i.e., why we ended up where we currently are. However, that story must remain open to further challenge and modification.

Structuring the current context. (Note here that ISO 31000 in fact does emphasize setting the context.) Neustadt-May asserts that the current context could/should be developed under three headings: 1) What is known? 2) What is unclear? and 3) What is presumed? It is important that the current situation be framed in that way to explicitly address the issues of uncertainty, information limitations, and assumptions.

When the current context has been described in the categories of what is known, unclear, and presumed, the next step at this stage is to ask/answer:

- What is the problem/challenge/issue?
- Whose problem/challenge/issue is it?

The purpose of these two questions is obvious, but there is a subtext. A process of examining the background narrative and the current context leads to a more insightful framing of the problem in question (rather than allowing the problem to frame the understanding of the past and present). Less evidently, focusing on the second question allows a more explicit recognition of the politics of decision-making inside the organization as a social system. Perceptions of risk can be considered here, as can the process issues related to organizational decision-making. This second question may also serve the role of detecting the location and availability of critical resources.

The next step is an identification of the desired outcomes of the defined problem. What result would satisfy the key stakeholders, or at least meet the minimum tests of acceptability? Obviously, this would include the development of relevant decision criteria. This stage of analysis also includes an assessment step. Is our description of the current context accurate? It may also be relevant here to consider what Neustadt and May call the 'analogous past.' Are there circumstances here or elsewhere that may provide us with guidance—particularly with respect to how similar situations have turned out.

Framing a decision/response. The third stage of the Neustadt-May process involves organizing some decision and resulting responsive actions in a rational form. The specifics of this stage are largely predicated on the particular aspects of the issues in question. However, Neustadt and May argue that the framing of a decision that leads to subsequent actions should include:

- A listing of the options.
- Assigning the odds associated with each option ('soft' or 'hard' odds).
- Recognition of the uncertainty and the unknown associated with both the options and the process of framing the options.

While this may resemble a somewhat conventional decision process,[5] Neustadt-May further identify several points in the analysis where assumptions are questioned and the process itself is held up to critical review. This feature of the process is wholly consonant with the points made previously: uncertainty, attitudes toward risk, subjective risk perceptions, and cognitive limitations matter—and they matter a lot.

A couple of final notes are important here. Economists tend to frame decision analysis in a manner that compels the elements of the problem to be monetized. Even preferences and attitudes are converted to monetary values or use surrogate monetary measures. However, there are fundamental and practical problems with this economics-based cost and benefit approach. Simply put, many costs and benefits cannot be monetized. This, of course, is problematic for a risk manager because the 'messy bits' may be the key elements to comprehend and understand regarding a risk or the uncertain elements around the current situation.

The principal benefit of a Neustadt-May perspective is that it forces consideration of the non-economic factors up to the front of the analysis. But, by doing so, the process promotes serious consideration of the need to formalize or order the thinking about the non-economic dimensions of risk management decisions. And this actually brings us back to our initial comments here. The essence of Neustadt-May is to formalize critical (slow) thinking and to embed it in the process of thinking about—well—in this case, risk management and in particular the important behavioral aspects associated with the interpretation and handling of emergent risks and uncertainties.

Add to this the possibility of including fast thinking or current insights from the organizational grape vines and surrounding stakeholders, for example, by utilizing simple techniques to map and analyze alternative perceptions that may differ from the predominant views of the central decision-makers.[6] There is ample evidence that reliance on a few experts at the center to guide us can lead to highly skewed predictions, whereas the consideration of multiple and diverse views from the center and the periphery provide more updated and reliable insights.[7]

Approaching uncertainty and unknowability management

The SDSTA Board viewed its charge as presenting nothing but uncertainties and unknowns. Indeed, only a few phenomena were remotely characterized as risks; for example:

- Workers' compensation data on mine safety.
- Engineering data on elevator functionality and shaft integrity.
- Insurance-based fire and other peril loss data for surface structures.

This limited risk information is, perhaps, a bit atypical of large projects but here it underscores our view that at the executive and board level, uncertainties dominate. How to proceed?

As we have stated, managers are confronted by a global business environment that is highly complex and interconnected so as to increase the level of uncertainty, and in many situations making it harder to forecast meaningfully. This seems to call for other risk management capabilities than those prescribed by the conventional frameworks based on the principles of identification, assessment, mitigation/handling, and monitoring. If the surroundings are becoming increasingly unpredictable, it is *not* possible in any meaningful way to identify all the major uncertainties, or uncertain situations, in advance to subsequently assess them, mitigate the effects, and then monitor and manage them. That is, the generic risk management cycle so centrally embedded in the ERM frameworks no longer makes sense—or in many cases is insufficient or irrelevant—it cannot do a proper job preparing an organization for the unexpected events that will occur sooner or later.

In fact, let us be clear, the trust in the conventional risk management tools can itself be a source of problems (recall, the 2008 crisis). If we rely on a set of risk management processes that try to handle the events we can predict in advance, we are indulging ourselves in a false sense of security, because we are unguarded against the uncertain, unexpected, unpredictable types of events that characterize dynamic complex systems.

When we are confronted with uncertainty, the best we presumably can do is to be observant and attempt to critically observe and interpret what we see to be happening around us—and try to react faster than competitors—in a business context, anyway—with proper and timely responses. But, we also need mechanisms and capabilities in place, probably engrained within the cultural fabric of the organization, that engage all relevant people by creating an inquisitive process to determine what the next most likely direction will be and then proposing/deciding on the next best steps. Such a set of processes could take much inspiration from the thinking around *exploratory options*—options on options—that allow the organization to investigate alternative routes forward without making excessive and premature commitments.

In a truly unpredictable environment, the only way to determine what might work going forward is to experiment—trying out what works, since most directed innovation investments will fail to hit the moving target. All of this sounds like we think this is rather easy and straightforward to accomplish—but of course—we do not. In reality only a very few organizations are able to accomplish this, and then only rarely for extended periods of time.

The following box gives you a reminder of how to deal with uncertainty and the unexpected.

A reminder: Dealing with uncertainty and the unexpected in a *world full of surprises!*

- **Risk**—try to be lucky, but adopt systematic approaches to deal with predictable risk events (eliminate, mitigate, transfer, manage) and thereby reduce uncertainty.
- Uncertainty—prepare for potential future scenarios and possible changes and form an alert responsive organization managed by open and collaborative individuals.
- **Unknowability**—we cannot know everything the future will bring, so we must search through innovation and small exploratory risk-taking probes to create options for adaptive moves.

How can we better observe new things evolving and hope to make sense of them? How can we structure decision-making and information processing to generate timely responses? How can we integrate updated observations with ongoing decisions considered to achieve the overarching corporate goals?

First, we think, we have to recognize that there are things we cannot control, which obviously is a challenge in a largely control-based ERM environment, and then prepare for the unexpected. In this regard, we can probably learn from some of the insights uncovered from studies of the so-called high-reliability organizations (HROs).[8] These organizations comprise entities that simply 'must not' fail—high risk ventures, e.g., nuclear powered submarines, aircraft carriers, fire brigades, electricity routers/dispatchers, etc. They have been studied in some detail as a special class of institutions with a peculiar set of behaviors that often enable them to avoid facing disaster from risks events gone awry.

The next box lists the common traits of HROs.

The common traits of high reliability organizations (HROs)

1. They are sensitive to operations.
2. People are constantly aware of how processes and systems may affect the organization and individuals pay close attention to operations and are aware about what is not working right.
3. They are reluctant to accept 'simple' explanations.
4. People resist simplifications and simple explanations, and everyone recognizes the consequences of generalizing and failing to understand the details and the real source of a problem.
5. They have a strong preoccupation with failure.
6. Employees at all levels in the organization are encouraged to think of ways the work processes can break down in a constant sense of shared attentiveness.
7. They respect expertise and listen to experts.
8. The decision-makers listen to the people who have the most developed knowledge and updated insights about the issues at hand.
9. They are resilient and generate solutions.
10. The leaders are prepared to respond to failures and continuously find or facilitate the development of new solutions to unexpected events.

Dealing with unknowable conditions, as the business environment evolves in a non-linear, irreversible, and path-dependent way, requires different skills and capabilities than dealing with risks. Some refer to them as more or less esoteric social constructs like dynamic capabilities[9] building on sequential elements of 'sensing,' 'seizing,' and 're-structuring' that allow the organization to identify opportunities and thereby enable it to adapt to the changing conditions. Or, strategic response capabilities or strategic responsiveness,[10] which require early observance of evolving events, ongoing sense-making, and an ability to generate responses in a timely way to deal with the events, so the organization at any given time can achieve the best fit with the prevailing environmental conditions.

This may possibly be achieved through the establishment of organization structures that can at the same time accommodate local responsiveness—meaning, that local actors can respond—and central coordination of general corporate actions, which in turn can be interpreted as an interactive *fast* and *slow* information processing system. Since we cannot foresee what will happen, we must be alert and see how things evolve in the fast system—typically as field observations from the operating entities at the edge of the organization—in ways that generate updated information and insights as a foundation for developing good integrated responses in the slow system at the corporate center/headquarters. Good responses to complex situations will often require collective solutions, because finding the optimal solution defies the capability of even the smartest and most intelligent individuals.

So, an extended version of *risk management* should support critical thinking (indeed, should *be* critical thinking) but will also require updated information from engaged knowledgeable individuals operating inside—or around the organizational periphery—that see new things happen and evolve before anyone else. All the while, there must be a willingness in the central administration, and among top management, to both being challenged and accepting the insights provided by lower ranking individuals—often the true experts—in the organization (see trait #4 of HROs). Here in this final sentence, we think we have hit the nail on the head. Human behavior typically defines—and/or defies—the challenge.

Imagining the interaction of risk and uncertainty within organizations

The SDSTA Board had to—at some moment—begin an early process of identifying risks and uncertainties but to do so without much in the way of technical expertise. To put it another way, this had to be a judgment-based risk assessment exercise. In this case, that proved to be easier said than done. One approach could be to follow a standardized checklist for risk assessment (they abound in the risk management world), but the sense of uniqueness with the situation led the Board and supporting individuals to adopt a version of a more instinctively useful approach, which we offer in a slightly stylized and conceptually framed way here.

Individuals within an organization (or, sometimes, within society itself) are the essential unit of measure. Their presence is intended to be a constant reminder that their perceptions, beliefs, and behaviors are first-order sources of risk and uncertainty. None of us has perfect knowledge, and awareness of that fact can lead us into a different frame of reference. To provide some shape to this notion, we present an idea that we think may take us some way toward rethinking the presence and impact of risk and uncertainty in/on organizations. Consider this.

An organization is the result of—in some cases many—years of conscious and rational, spontaneous, opportunistic, and required/ unavoidable human interactions entered into between leaders, managers, and employees and various organizational resource holders. *Resource holders* is a term that refers to a wide range of (largely but not exclusively external) stakeholders and stakeholder interests, such as investors, regulators, funding agencies, customers, suppliers, partners, surrounding communities, the climate, and so forth. These arrangements mainly serve the declared purposes of the organization, but sometimes impose purposes on that organization as well (say a legal mandate or regulatory requirement). For explanatory purposes the human interactions between stakeholders can be categorized as contracts, obligations, commitments, or agreements. This framework has some relationship to the so-called contractarian view of organizations, but we think it moves beyond that more restrictive view.

- **Contracts** are *legally enforceable* arrangements that meet the ordinary tests of offer and acceptance, consideration, legality of purpose, and legal capacity.
- **Obligations** refer to *legally binding* arrangements that are required of an organization and, typically, are not the fruit of party/counterparty offer and acceptance. A legal statute would be an example to reflect that.
- **Commitments** typically convey *self-imposed duties*. The duty of present generations to future generations is often cited in current debates about social security and environmental concerns and constitute good illustrations of a commitment. Moral and ethical values represent pervasive commitments. The principal governing characteristic of commitments is that only a single party need be

involved in the formation and implementation of a commitment—
though obviously a commitment affects others.

- **Agreements** may often enjoy legal enforceability, like contracts
  and obligations, but the term is intended to connote *less formal
  arrangements* between parties that may fall somewhat outside a
  legal sphere. Politically motivated agreements between communities
  to advance a particular purpose illustrate the non-legal dimension
  of agreements. It can also be reflected in expectations expressed by
  leaders in corporate values—or codes of conduct—imposed on the
  organization and its members, the (actually) practiced values and
  rewards systems, etc. Oh yes, and we would also include 'friendships'
  in this category.
- **Arrangements** are the glue that binds together the social building
  blocks of organizations, and—we would argue—might be seen as an
  integral part of that organization's *exposure to uncertainty* reflecting
  the fact that an organization assumes an incremental exposure
  to uncertainty as the human interactions play out in concrete
  actions. Add to this the concepts of 'trust' and 'reputation,' where
  organizations—more or less consciously—may develop strong and
  durable stakeholder connections creating a good standing reputation
  as a reliable counterpart through concrete actions. These network
  relationships can be very helpful when unexpected events happen as
  the means to find collaborative solutions to complex circumstances.

Yet, the human interactions can also have negative and often unrecognized
effects (they may particularly go unnoticed in informal values-based
arrangements that work under the radar) caused by potential biases,
psychological shortcomings, or self-interested political behaviors. They
can also have positive effects in organizations that foster cultures of
open sharing of risk information and collaborative deliberations about
better solutions to new or emergent risk challenges. The risks that arise
from the entire risk management field, comprised by directly measurable
exposures as well as related behavioral effects, can be collectively defined
and referred to as the organization's *uncertainty profile*; in some narrow
circumstances, *risk profile* might be employed.

To explain, these interactive forms—let us refer to them generally, and
more appropriately, as *relationships*—can create incremental risks and
uncertainties for the organization and they may serve as portals to deal
more effectively with risk or uncertainty. For example, an employment
contract will specify certain contractual matters that are unique to that
contract, say salary, job duties, measures of performance, and so on. In that

sense, the contract is creating expectations, duties, and rights that have enforceability. Absent the formal contract, the organization would not explicitly encounter the associated risks or uncertainty. The employment contract might also allow external risks/uncertainties to pass through to the organization. For example, the workers' compensation and employers' liability laws exist independently of individual employment contracts, but by entering into an employment contract, the organization becomes exposed to legal expectations associated with, e.g., providing safe working conditions for employees. Yet, many of the most important relationships between leaders, managers, and employees may take the form of more informal commitments and unwritten agreements often enforced by subtle moral values enforced through the influence of an organizational culture.

These relationships can further be characterized by the presence of possible risk/uncertainty-distributing characteristics. A commitment to some moral value does not permit risk distribution, as it is a self-imposed duty. However, a multiparty contract with vendors may create numerous opportunities for distribution. Consider here that risk-distribution—whether in the form of insurance, derivative contracts, or other contractual means—is an attempt to 'trade' specified risk exposures among different parties at a 'fair' price (data may help us determine appropriate premiums) and thereby diversify the collective exposures across more shoulders. If this is done 'fair and square' it might not be in conflict with moral values. It will, however, be in conflict with moral values if the risk-distribution entails a 'manipulated' transfer that creates negative economic externalities, e.g., by using public resources (for free) that will threaten the environment.

Relatedly Nassim Taleb argues that "corporate managers have incentives without disincentives," i.e., in many publicly listed corporations, executive stock option schemes provide incentives that favor short-term economizing behaviors at the expense of investing in longer-term sustainability efforts. This can make large public companies vulnerable over time as Taleb argues: "they eventually collapse under the weight of the agency problem, while managers milk them for bonuses and ditch the bones to taxpayers."[11] In other words, the way corporate decision-makers are incentivized can 'manipulate' risk transfer because they can gain from short-term upside gains without any repercussions to longer-term downside effects that must be assumed by (corporate pension funds or) society at large. These are governance-driven arrangements and therefore carry legal authority, i.e., they comply with prevailing law, but they are devoid of concerns for fairness and moral values. We might call this the 'other people's money' problem.

From the perspective of a so-called rational power (or economic forces) assessment, the distribution and transfer of risk would seem to be a function of some, if not all, of the following:

- The number of parties to the relationship.
- The relative negotiating strength or leverage of the parties.
- The legal or moral enforceability of the relationship.
- The risk-bearing capacity of the parties.
- The relationship of a particular arrangement with other relationships.
- The influence of external interests (i.e., external to the specific relationship).

Add to this, however, that managing the 'irrational' non-contractual values-based relationships may have very forceful impacts on the ability to manage important long-term exposures in an uncertain evolving world. For example, the fact that A. P. Møller–Mærsk decided to build double hull tankers after the Exxon Valdez ran aground in Alaska in 1989 and switch the entire fleet within an impressive four-year period long before other shipping companies (and ahead of the US Oil Pollution Act of 1990 (OPA 90) that required a gradual phase-out over a 20-year period 1995–2015) was probably a conscious and quite rational decision.

While the company did not recover the sizeable investment initially, it was considered the 'right thing to do,' and it brought the company ahead of the game when a faster phase-out scheme was implemented later after the oil tanker Erika capsized off the French Atlantic coast in December 2000 creating an ecological disaster.[12] So, in this case, taking the morally right decision turned out to be both smart and timely and allowed the company to make adjustments to (eventually inevitable) legal requirements in the making. At the same time, the move increased the corporate reputation as a trusted corporate relationship, which could be used later to deal with messy complex challenges that required collaborative solutions with various external stakeholders.

Relatedly, there is evidence to suggest that the ability to engage in fast responses after major events is more effective than waiting for, say, insurance reimbursement for claims on direct losses. Hence, installing responsive organizational structures and processes can be more beneficial for economic recovery than replacement of assets,[13] particularly when embedded in dynamic networks.[14]

Finally, as it appears—these relationships have a history, and while the process of risk assessment tends to focus its efforts on describing what exists and how it might be managed, there is always value in understanding why the relationships exist in the first place. One of the challenging complications of this view of risk management is that it forces the matter of 'interdependencies' (and history) into the forefront of analysis. If the relationships or interdependencies between these exposures are too strong, statistical analysis diminishes in its power to predict and measure. And, as we have already stated, managers are mainly dealing with uncertainties anyway.

The irony of the limitation of quantification is that it tends to encourage risk managers to view long-term interdependency as a nuisance to be assumed away or controlled for in analysis, whereas our view plainly states that interdependencies are the very point— or at least a key point—in understanding the dynamic effects of risk management in organizations. These relationships are entered into, more or less, intentionally (although often informally and unobserved), and they are expected to serve a common mission or set of purposes for which the organization exists. It would, in this light, be absurd not to wonder about the interrelatedness of risks and uncertainties as they are displayed in these relationships. So, when we analyze the risks or uncertainties around a particular relationship, it must be understood that each contract, obligation, commitment, agreement, and/or 'friendly' association—possibly enforced by trust and reputation—is expected to, at least potentially, have an impact on all the other relationships.

Interestingly—and usefully—in the case of the SDSTA/SURF story, it was through a recognition that relationships were central to the risk management imagery, that the laboratory's relationship with the local Native American population (Lakota) came to be more clearly seen as highly critical, permeating almost every aspect of the project.

A FEW OTHER THINGS TO CONSIDER

If asked where we would expect the most push-back on our views, it probably would come from those who have invested time, treasure, and mental effort in promoting further extension and sophistication of measures to quantify risk. So—for a final time—we are motivated to be as clear as we can about our views on 'that thing we are hoping to manage.'

Nothing we have asserted in this book should be seen as a diminishment of the importance of improving our technical and quantitative efforts to measure uncertainty, thereby turning uncertainties into risks. Four hundred years of insurance-industry success should tell us something important—there are phenomena in our world that can be observed, analyzed, measured and can lead to the creation of reasonable estimates of future outcomes. The same can be said of other market-based risks, which are the meat-and-potatoes of financial risk management. As Peter Bernstein has argued in his highly regarded book, *Against the Gods: The Remarkable Story of Risk*, one of the key things that separates the modern world from the ancient is our ability to measure risk—and we believe that too.[15] Medical science is illustrative of other areas where the analysis of risk has proved to matter greatly. And, the Artificial Intelligence and Big Data movements hold the promise of salutary effects on our ability to discern patterns and insights in an uncertain world.

Still, even in highly sophisticated risk markets we would do well to remember the old saying that markets run on fear and greed. In the case of the insurance market, we might slightly amend that to say that mistakes (good and bad) drive the underwriting cycle. Those mistakes may be due to fear or greed, but we would have to add caution and overconfidence into the mix of root causes. As for wider financial markets, well, 2008 was not due merely to technical glitches in modeling—as we fairly thoroughly argued. Even highly and accurately measurable situations can fall prey to basic human instincts, limitations, and behaviors.

However, you will not find us on the opposite shore from those that believe the pursuit of ever more precise estimates of 'measurable uncertainty' is a worthy aspiration. It is. But it needs to be understood that the emphasis on *risk* as the central feature of our field of study and practice has flipped what we believe is the more proper view—which is that the focus of emphasis must be on *uncertainty* and *unknowability*, as they are the more prominent features we encounter.

It is also worth keeping in mind that the quest for better ways to measure unmeasurable *uncertainty* has its limitations and may carry within it the risk of applying complex methods and complicated imagery where they do not belong. Or, in the words of Nassim Taleb: "What is nonmeasurable and nonpredictable will remain nonmeasurable and unpredictable, no matter how many PhDs with Russian and Indian names you put on the job—and no matter how much hate mail I get."[16]

... and further

All the ERM frameworks have at their core a generic risk management cycle of risk identification, risk assessment, risk mitigation/handling, and risk monitoring—this serves a purpose and works well in the context of—obviously—risk. The reason is that measurability is based on historic events that can vouch for a reasonable degree of repeatability going forward, which allows us to assign meaningful probabilities to future events. No problem—we have no *qualms* with that approach—it works quite well in the case of risk.

However, there are two major challenges to this approach:

1. If we believe that all the risk information processed and reported in the formal ERM approach is accurate and managed rationally by the many people/decision-makers involved, we are making a big mistake. The interpretation of the risk information and the human reasoning that extend from it is exposed to many psychological pitfalls.
2. If we apply the methodology to deal with uncertainty and unknowable circumstances, we are bound to make mistakes by measuring something that is by nature unmeasurable—and using this as a basis for important decisions is bound to get it wrong.

Creating conscious awareness about these two challenges is obviously essential for the ability to find better ways to deal with them. They are not new revelations, but their importance seems to have accelerated significantly in recent years as the conventional risk management view is gaining a stronger foothold in dominating our thinking.

Dealing with the first challenge is not new; with known recipes like being open, listening to others, engaging in inquisitive discussions, etc. However, the issues go much deeper than we think and delve into subtle issues like culturally borne values and ethical dimensions going all the way to the top echelons of the organization. We have humbly suggested a number of possible inroads to deal more explicitly with this, e.g., by analyzing the human 'relationships' around essential stakeholders, using historical narratives to uncover informational 'noise' and 'biases,' checking values in practice against espoused values, etc. We are hopeful that something can be done to alleviate these issues but do not really have high expectations. The reality is, that we are likely to see these phenomena repeat themselves again and again over time. But at least we should no longer be surprised when ERM compliant organizations encounter issues grounded in human flaws.

Dealing with the second challenge is not really new either with techniques like scenario planning—in various forms—developed and for long applied exactly with the purpose of preparing decision-makers for highly uncertain and unpredictable future contexts often as part of a developed risk management process. Yet, we see regularly that such programs are being discontinued in organizations often due to changes at the highest governance level almost as an inevitable law of human systems. We have humbly suggested that thinking about smarter ways to process updated environmental risk information in 'open' exchanges between the people in the trenches—that is, the daily operators—and the senior executives in the organization could be a useful practice. But, despite potential goodwill, this is extremely difficult to implement and only rarely occurs in real organizations—although the best of them can achieve it, it is just not called *risk management.*

Add to this the idea the ERM frameworks continue to assume a top-down driven strategy-making process with clear and unambiguous long-term objectives to be achieved—typically developed for the Executive Committee and approved by the Board of Directors. It also assumes that the governance layer (the top management team and the board members) is able to express an unambiguous risk appetite statement that can guide all the resource-committing decisions made throughout the organization. This sounds a little naïve—even irrational—in a turbulent world, where the ability to adapt the organization's business activities to the changing circumstances should be a key concern in risk management. But the expressly stated purpose of ERM is still to help accomplish the once-stated strategic objectives, come what may. In many cases these goals turn out to be simple and overambitious growth and earnings targets that may force employees to do unethical things they otherwise would not do (just think about the Dieselgate debacle). This is obviously not an intended effect, we hope, but it nonetheless happens. Is it now time to call for a more nuanced purpose for risk management, such as, helping organizational decision-makers *think* about the potential future consequences of major commitments?

We can improve risk management by being more conscious about the 'human factors' in the process—the psychological pitfalls—that demonstrably have such dramatic impacts. We should think more about how we think about risk—and facilitate more conscious decision-making considering the full spectrum of the organizational *risk profile* and the evolving *risk landscape.*

Do we really need to integrate everything to do that? Enterprise-wide integration was a neat idea fostered by insights about diversification effects from financial portfolio theory, but we also need dedicated focus and expertise to handle specific risk functions.

We can improve organizational responsiveness by adding fast information processing to the system, where the updated insights of people engaged in the daily operations—the early signals—are channeled to the strategic reasoning performed around top management. And feedback to the organization can provide current and relevant guidance to the business activities, so operating managers can respond meaningfully to observed changes in the local task environments. Interaction as opposed to integration then seems to be at the essence of effective risk management.

Ideally, this can form the basis for ongoing interactions between fast (operational) and slow (executive) forward-looking thinking where the fast-slow interaction forms a dynamic adaptive system that allows the organization to adapt activities to changes in the environment.[17] In a future risk landscape characterized by higher degrees of unknowability with a potential for extreme outcomes, this seems to be the essence of what we suppose we must refer to as risk management.

Many of the emerging exposures are well beyond the scope of individual organizations with broader societal effects—maybe even dealing with the sustainability of mankind.[18] This seems to call for the ability to generate collaborative solutions engaging broad stakeholder involvement—an approach that goes well beyond the confines of a control-based risk management program aimed to generate optimal returns and achieving stated strategic objectives.

EXTENDED SUMMARY

Our first chapter is titled 'Is this a risk management book?' Our answer is yes, IF we define risk management as follows:

> Risk management is an aspect of generalized management and leadership that is focused on understanding and responding to the impacts of uncertainty, the unknown, and—yes—where possible risk on an organization and its stakeholders. This reorientation places primary emphasis on understanding humans perceiving and behaving in an uncertain world and thus means that it is fundamentally a 'moral' exercise. Because it is a moral exercise, and because we are dealing with the uncertain and the unknown more often than we are dealing with risk, critical thinking is of paramount importance. And because we believe this to be true, the essential purpose or goal of risk management is to support the development of sustainably resilient organizations.

Of course, a predictable response might well be, 'so what?' Does this actually affect the practice of risk management/leadership in organizations? We have already argued that many of the technical aspects of risk management are not under indictment here. Organizations will/ should still buy insurance, introduce safety and security measures, rely on financial risk tools, and more. What does fundamentally change, however, is the orientation of our *thinking* about risk management as a field of study and practice. As it turns out, this changes the whole meaning and purpose. And importantly we think it changes what risk managers/leaders do with their time.

To a significant degree, the development of our view is based on the striking discrepancy between the stringent rational approach outlined in the formal ERM frameworks—that permeate the official descriptions of the risk management processes—and then what we observe in practice; what the organizations really do. We acknowledge that there are arguments to be made that this gap is simply evidence that the ERM idea takes time and that things will really take off when organizations reach maturity. We believe there is certainly something to that but consider the situation a bit differently.

One of the—let us say it, notorious—features of academic research is that moment when a scholar needs to think carefully about variables to include in an analysis and variables that are excluded or—perhaps—held constant. The risk of course is that an effort to get a meaningful result within the research method may screen out information that either tells a different story or blocks out the ability to see interactive effects in action. It is always a tricky thing, but we are reminded of that dilemma when we think about the gap between espoused ERM and ERM in practice. Because the researcher's thinking and the model itself may be the problem, we are inclined to wonder whether an alternative explanation is in play here. Could it be that the gap is evidence that the model itself is limited in its ability to tell us what risk management is? We are definitely leaning toward that explanation, and simply state that at some point the mounting number of things that do not fit into the model begin to tell us more about the model than anything else.

This is a hard thesis to argue and reminds us (only a little) of Galileo, where the fundamental premise on which so much belief, effort, and practice hangs is called into question. At the end of the day, we are not particularly ambitious to change the world; we are interested in presenting an alternative view and asking for consideration of the ideas we set forward. But, just to be clear that we really do believe what we are saying, consider the following points as suggestions that the ERM model needs to be questioned:

- The risk management process in organizations is *often* driven by the efforts of unique individuals in unique situations.
- The emphasis on a risk management process is *often* triggered by an unexpected crisis situation (or near-death organizational experience).
- The risk management focus is *often* gradually or abruptly ended due to changes at the governance level (complacency, new CEO, power plays, firing rounds, etc.).

- The risk management process is good at handling small 'nitty gritty' risks, but *often* misses the really *big* risks that can 'make or break' the organization.
- The risk information processing (reporting) is *often* influenced by people that package and interpret the contents (groups, functions, management layers).
- The use of reported risk information is *often* negatively affected by various psychological—we might also say political—pitfalls of decision-makers.
- The major risk (disaster) incidents *often* entail ethical issues and flaws at the highest organizational governance levels.

In other words, what is actually happening may not align with expectations because 'something else is going on.' And, it seems, what is going on is that risk management is an aspect of management and leadership as practiced by *people* in organizations, is affected by all sorts of human shortcomings and, therefore—and this should not really surprise us—it does *not* resemble the neat and rationalized processes outlined in the formal ERM frameworks. And here is our point of departure—neither, particularly, should it.

One version of this book would begin wrapping up about now; here are our ideas, what do you think? In deciding to do this, however, we need to realize that some of the issues we raise could not be reduced to a simple illustrative solution.

For example, the challenge of obtaining top-level buy-in to begin and support a wide-ranging approach to risk management remains possibly the most vexing issue in modern risk management. Given some of the insights we offered, this is a very tough nut to crack. Risk management has always suffered from what we might call the 'eat your peas' syndrome. The mindset change necessary is daunting as it requires individuals to fundamentally reorient their view of the world to one where we understand that assessing and addressing risk, uncertainty, and the unknown is something fundamental to the world we inhabit and that while complexity reigns, there are constructive ways of approaching the challenge that can have collective and positive effects on organizational performance and well-being. In stating this, we are very aware that this sounds like weak tea, but it actually underscores the fact that understanding human psychology and behavior is a core aspect of risk management as we see it. Think about how often those subjects appear in conventional risk management training and education programs (hint: not much) and you begin to see part of the problem—we are ignoring or holding constant perhaps the most influential factor in risk management.

Other issues to which we cannot provide an adequately robust solution? Let us try thinking about time. Can we actually and meaningfully operate with a full recognition of the long run?

We raised this issue much earlier in the book, but it is still here—lingering just out of sight. Of course, there is a long run in the metaphysical sense. Our question here is asked at a more earth-bound level. Can organizations behave with a firmly embedded and resolute commitment to a long-range vision/aim and a commitment toward achieving sustainable long-term outcomes? Just contrast this with the short-term nature of common incentives on Wall Street—do whatever it takes to earn a fortune now, then retire in Florida, and leave the consequences to whomever is still left on board.

Cultural anthropologists have noted that social cultures present differing views of the future or time itself, and some seem to have a longer-range orientation than others. Business research shows that certain social cultures can influence or orient strategic thinking toward more distant time horizons. But we think everyday evidence shows that commitment to the long run is a struggle for most humans and organizations. It is achievable, yes, but...

Why does this matter here? Risk management—even as we look at it—engages in issues of time at a fundamental level. This is not a new insight, and even early writing on risk management noticed that the time dimension feature of risk management investments can really challenge managers. This is for the simple fact that many (if not most) risk management measures require immediate or early investment, while pay-offs only happen over time (as in the example of A. P. Møller–Mærsk) and, even then, only probabilistically.

So, one of the issues here is what we might call the 'apple-to-oranges' comparison. Psychologically, the present and the future are not equal in meaning or value. As noted earlier, we in the business and economics fields have enshrined this idea in the concept of 'time value of money,' which, if we think about it, carries with it a certain orientation toward valuing the present over the future.

But let us put this issue at a more basic level. As we have seen in our numerous illustrations, a successful ERM program does not necessarily lead to a long-term commitment to ERM within organizations. Things change, leaders change, strategies change, and otherwise successful ERM programs sometimes disappear before our very eyes. Clinically, an answer might be that the organization did not take the necessary steps to embed ERM into the organization culture, but it very well might be that deeper and subtle human forces are at work—including various psychological pitfalls—so yes, long-term commitments may be inherently difficult to make and adhere to.

Furthermore, recall from previous discussion that this is not a public sector versus a private sector issue. Various influences impede the public sector from making long-term investments in infrastructure, emergency response, disaster recovery, and other efforts that involve short-term investment/long-term reward. Indeed, the illustrations where the time horizon has been overcome stand out by their rarity. In the US, for example, the Social Security system and the national highway system illustrate that success is possible, and each might teach us something about managing against the long run. At the center of both achievements are stories of exemplary political acumen and a recognition that the biggest obstacle is to think too big. Just getting started seems to be a key (while the leadership must hold the bigger vision firmly in mind). This has, we think, something to do with the old sales adage: 'it is easier to sell something than to sell the idea of that something.'

What, then, to do about this? In our more fatalistic moments we would be inclined to say: 'Do what you can do, risk managers/leaders, but don't waste a lot of time thinking about the long-term impacts of your work.' We do not feel good about saying that, however, so the suggestion is to recognize the immense difficulty of developing long-term commitments and then to recognize that focusing on short-term issues that initiate a potentially long-term commitment is possible the best way of thinking. 'Embedding' and sustaining a long-term commitment seems only possible at a deep cultural level, which itself takes time. It can happen, but there is not a long track record of success!

A rose by any other name ...

So, what are we to call this thing we have been discussing? If we are not mainly managing *risk* but are dealing more with *uncertainty* and *unknowability*, then is it right to call it *risk management*? Well, despite begging off in Chapter 1, we were eventually going to have to come back to this—is *risk management* the right name for what we are describing? We are mindful that business professors are notorious for seeking out (and finding!) new words, catchphrases, and imagery that, with a roll of the dice, become the next big thing. And, by the way, we do not necessarily mean that in the positive sense. Nevertheless, let us make a go of it.

At the outset we must acknowledge that—as in so many things—Shakespeare beat us to the punch. The name is not the thing. And we could apply the same logic to risk management. Naming our view of 'the thing' is not as critical as describing what it is, and why it is important. Nevertheless, we think we need to produce at least an arguable suggestion. We choose Strategic Risk Leadership. This puts us out on a limb and we are not entirely comfortable doing so. Certainly we claim no possession rights to the term and are somewhat unsettled at the thought of unintentionally becoming known as 'the strategic risk leadership guys.'

Strategic Risk Leadership (OK, let us also establish the acronym, SRL) has some limitations, but we think too it presents at least a few defensible benefits. First, the application of the word *strategic* places our arguments in the framework of an overarching view of where assessing and addressing risk/uncertainty/the unknown should be positioned in the life of the organization. While the term often is associated with the highest levels of an organization, it also connotes planning, looking into the future (near and distant), adopting an organization-wide orientation, and demonstrating a sense of openness in seeking to comprehend the impacts of the uncertain future. In that sense, *strategic* can apply to any manager anywhere in an organization.

Second, *leadership* seems to suggest an important point that undergirds a significant part of our book. Yes, there are managerial dimensions to the work we describe but, more often than not, risk/uncertainty/the unknown puts us in the position of having to address challenges where we do not have the authority or autonomy to produce a command-and-control response; where we have to collaborate with others; or where through persuasion, encouragement, or education we promote critical thinking and critical action in the face of an uncertain world.

Well that is two arguments for the term SRL. The weak spot in our phrase is, of course, *risk*, for the obvious reason that risk is not the number one matter of importance to us. Here we simply concede to convention—*uncertainty* is probably the term most consistent with our view. And someday we might change our minds to argue for Strategic Uncertainty Management, but frankly, we do not think either of us has the energy for taking that on right now.

There. We feel better having written the preceding four paragraphs. Yes, Strategic Risk Leadership will do. When we describe a function or an activity that is based on recognizing the centrality of critical thinking in response to a world of uncertainty, when we think about the need to understand human behavior and to engage with humans as the central 'unit of measure,' when we recognize that seeking cultural change and a moral center to the work we undertake, and when we aspire to lead our organization toward a sustainable and resilient footing—well—that sounds like Strategic Risk Leadership fits the bill.

NOTES

1   Halberstam, David (1972). *The Best and the Brightest*. Random House, New York.
2   The SURF story is extracted from Young, P.C. (May 2019). *The Sanford Underground Research Facility: Testing the Limits of the Enterprise Risk Management Concept*. The Case Centre.
3   The source document for this methodology is T. Dean Maines (2011). Self-assessment and improvement process for organizations, in Bouckaert and Zsolnai (eds.). *The Palgrave Handbook of Spirituality and Business*.
4   Neustadt, Richard E. and May, Ernest R. (1986). *Thinking in Time: The Uses of History for Decision Makers (1st ed.)*. Free Press, New York.
5   Drucker, Peter F. (1967). The effective decision. *Harvard Business Review*, 45(1): 92–98.
6   See, for example,Gray, S., Chan, A., Clark, D. and Jordan, R. (2012). Modeling the integration of stakeholder knowledge in social-ecological decision-making: Benefits and limitations to knowledge diversity. *Ecological Modelling*, 229: 88–96.
7   Epstein, David (2019). The peculiar blindness of experts. The Atlantic. www.theatlantic.com/magazine/archive/2019/06/how-to-predict-the-future/588040/.
8   Weick, Karl E. and Sutcliffe, Kathleen M. (2001). *Managing the Unexpected: Assuring High Performance in an Age of Complexity*. Jossey-Bass, San Francisco, CA. Weick, Karl E. and Sutcliffe, Kathleen M. (2007). *Managing the Unexpected: Resilient in an Age of Uncertainty* (2nd ed.). Jossey-Bass, San Francisco, CA. Weick, Karl E. and Sutcliffe, Kathleen M. (2015). *Managing the Unexpected: Sustained Performance in a Complex World* (3rd ed.). Wiley, Hoboken, NJ. Nb—notice how the language (verbiage) changes over time.
9   See, e.g.,Helfat, C.E., Finkelstein, S., Mitchell, W., Peteraf, M., Singh, H., Teece, D. and Winter, S.G. (2009). *Dynamic Capabilities: Understanding Strategic Change in Organizations*. Wiley, Hoboken, NJ.
10 Andersen, T.J., Denrell, J. and Bettis, R.A. (2007). Strategic responsiveness and Bowman's risk–return paradox. *Strategic Management Journal*, 28(4): 407–429.
11 Taleb, Nassim Nicholas (2013). *Antifragile: Things that Gain from Disorder*. Penguin Books, Londo. (pp. 397 and 405).
12 Andersen, T.J. (2017). Corporate responsible behavior in multinational enterprise. *International Journal of Organizational Analysis* 25(3).
13 Hallegatte, S. and Dumas, P. (2009). Can natural disasters have positive consequences? Investigating the role of embodied technical change. *Ecological Economics*, 68 (3), 777–786.
14 Seville, E., Stevenson, J.R., Vargo, J., Brown, C. and Giovinazzi, S. (2015). Resilience and recovery: Business behavior following the Canterbury earthquakes. In Ayyub, B.M., Chapman, R.E., Galloway, G.E. and Wright, R.N. (eds.), *Economics of Community Disaster Resilience Workshop Proceedings*, NIST Special Publication 1600, National Institute of Standards and Technology (NIST), Washington, DC, 177–183.

15 Bernstein, Peter (1998). *Against the Gods: The Remarkable Story of Risk.* Wiley, New York.
16 Taleb, Nassim Nicholas (2013). *Antifragile: Things that Gain from Disorder.* Penguin Books, London (p. 138).
17 See, for example, Andersen, T.J. and Fredens, K. (2013). *The Responsive Organization. CGSR Working Paper Series No. 1*, Copenhagen Business School.
18 World Economic Forum (2018). *The Global Risk Report.*

Index

For Product Safety Concerns and Information please contact our EU
representative GPSR@taylorandfrancis.com Taylor & Francis Verlag GmbH,
Kaufingerstraße 24, 80331 München, Germany

Printed and bound by CPI Group (UK) Ltd, Croydon, CR0 4YY

01/05/2025

01858384-0001